**FAKE FOOD, SO PERFECT
IT LOOKS REAL; AND THE REAL FOOD,
SO PERFECT IT LOOKS FAKE**

**IN TOKYO
HOW CAN ANYBODY EVER
KNOW WHAT TO EAT?!**

Dedicated to the memory of
Jonathan Gold (1960-2018)

TIM ANDERSON

TOKYO
STORIES

Photography by Nassima Rothacker

Hardie Grant
BOOKS

THERE'S JUST NOWHERE QUITE LIKE IT.

7

Have you heard of Paris syndrome? Paris syndrome is a temporary mental condition that strikes when bitter disappointment and extreme culture shock collide on the Champs-Élysées. It refers to the emotional distress that can occur when one visits Paris for the first time and finds that it falls far, far short of expectations. Bad cases of Paris syndrome can apparently result in anxiety, tachycardia, paranoia, vomiting, hallucinations and even death. Wait, no, not death. But still! It's real and it's crazy. And I love Paris, but I can totally get how this could happen. I mean, can you imagine expecting – actually expecting – a glistening romantic fairytale wonderland like something out of *Moulin Rouge!* or *An American in Paris* and instead finding dirty streets filled with cynical tourist traps and second-hand smoke? How upsetting.

IT'S HARD TO IMAGINE THIS HAPPENING IN TOKYO.

There's no such thing as 'Tokyo syndrome', and if there were, it would probably be something awesome, like a fantastic psychedelic drug trip with no fuzzy after-effects. In fact, if Tokyo syndrome did exist, it would probably be the *opposite* of Paris syndrome. Tokyo is a city so overwhelmingly impressive that it can be hard to cope with, especially on your first visit. So you've been to London and you've been to New York and they're big and fabulous, but NO. They are like quaint provincial hamlets compared to Tokyo. But it's not just because Tokyo is big – it's also because Tokyo is *bonkers*. There's just no other city so reelingly vertical, so colourful, so fast-paced, so crowded and dense with diverting stimuli at every turn. (Except maybe Vegas. But Vegas wouldn't make for a very good cookbook.)

東
京

Tokyo

And no matter how wondrous and insane you expect Tokyo to be, it's highly unlikely that you'll be disappointed. Quite the contrary – you'll probably go to Tokyo thinking it'll be five stars – great city! But in actuality it's FIVE STARS! ★★★★★ AMAZING CITY!!!

AND THE FOOD. MY GOD, THE FOOD!

Many Japanese people and argumentative Japanophile nerds (don't give me that look) will tell you that Tokyo doesn't have the best food in Japan. And hey, they may be right. But even if they are, the food in Tokyo is still so good I can't conceive of anyone who might be disappointed there. That includes people who don't even like Japanese food, because that's not all Tokyo has to offer – it's also got some of the finest Italian pizza, Korean barbecue, Hawaiian *poke* and Austrian pastries in the world, to name but a few.

For a city with an immigrant population of (no joke) less than 0.2%, Tokyo is a remarkably cosmopolitan city in terms of cuisine. This is something I'll never quite understand, but if I had to guess, I'd say it's because Tokyoites live in a culture of forward-thinking innovation combined with a persistent tradition of craft and attention to detail. This combination produces some of the most interesting and delicious food on the planet, whether it's ramen, pizza or soft-serve ice cream.

In most cities, lowest-of-the-lowbrow food outlets, like convenience stores and vending machines, aren't places you'd expect to find good food, or even acceptable food. But soon after arriving in Tokyo, you'll find that's not the case in Japan. Vending machines sell, among other things, hundreds of varieties of invigorating tea, fresh dashi, crisp fried chicken, powerful highballs, and surprisingly delicious hot soups in little cans (so warming in the wintertime). Then there are the *conbini*, the ubiquitous convenience stores, always open and always nearby for when you need an umbrella, a tin of oxygen (for real), or a reliably delicious and cheap lunch. In all honesty, conbini may be the thing I miss most about Japan.

You can eat surprisingly well in Tokyo without even trying, just sticking to subway-station kiosks and fast-food chains. But dive a little deeper, and that's when Tokyo's incomparable deliciousness really begins to unfold. Follow your nose to find sweet and smoky *yakitori*, indulgent buttery pastries, comforting curries, or that liquid gold of rendered porcine alchemy known as *tonkotsu* ramen. Get to know the many varieties of bento, miniaturised Japanese feasts tidily contained in compact lunchboxes, which can provide an amazing array of new flavours. And if you're feeling flush, seek out some of Tokyo's fine dining, representing the best of the best of the BEST – whether it's sushi, Peking duck or French haute cuisine. Tokyo has it all.

But of course, with all of its fine food and bright lights and towering towers, it's easy to lose sight of the fact that for millions, Tokyo is simply home. For visitors, Tokyo is an amusement park; for residents, it's a daily routine. Tokyo is a place where people actually live, sometimes in the suburbs but sometimes right in the thick of it. And the home kitchens of Tokyo are places for respite from the crowds and the clamour, where the cooking is often simple and comforting, but still influenced by the city's impeccable produce and constantly-shifting cosmopolitan trends. If you live in Tokyo you'll likely have to contend with cooking in a tiny kitchen, but you'll also have access to some of the most exciting ingredients in the world.

This is a recipe book, of course, but it can also be used as a reference guide for a trip to Tokyo. Some recipes are directly inspired by specific restaurants in Tokyo, which are well worth checking out. Other dishes aren't based on anywhere specific, but I've included a recommendation for where to find an excellent version. But these are just my suggestions. Be sure to do your own research before a trip to Tokyo, with special attention to opening hours – restaurants often close on one random day of the week, so look these up ahead of time so you don't trek across town only to arrive at a closed restaurant! Hopefully you'll find the glossary on page 244 useful, too, whether you are cooking or travelling.

I've been to Tokyo eight times, and I never get bored of it – it always, *always* has something new in store to surprise and delight me. There are few cities in the world as dynamic and exciting and rewarding to explore, and I can't imagine there will ever come a time when I won't feel the need to return.

In fact, what are you doing next week?

I'M FREE!
AND FLIGHTS ARE CHEAP!

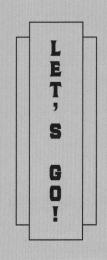

東京

A TYPICAL DAY ON A TRIP TO TOKYO

Start the day on a toilet more sophisticated than your car ¥ Snarf some stringy, sticky, smelly fermented soybeans (*natto*) for breakfast ¥ Get lost in the labyrinthine obstacle course of Shinjuku station ¥ Have a peaceful stroll around the Imperial Palace gardens ¥ Get lunch at a robot / maid / butler / cat / owl / Hello Kitty café ¥ Lose an hour (and several thousand yen) at one of Akihabara's multi-storey arcades ¥ Ogle the tourists and touristy tat along Nakamise-Dori ¥ Purchase some surprisingly beautiful hand-carved chopsticks and a bottle of fizzy *ramune* ¥ Kick off the evening with an 'all you can drink' lager deal ¥ Head to an *izakaya* and eat ALL THE FOOD ¥ Drink *shochu* ¥ Make friends ¥ Do karaoke ¥ Accidentally walk into a brothel ¥ Walk back out, quickly ¥ A little more shochu ¥ Ham sandwich from the conbini ¥ Hello again, fancy toilet! ¥ Bedtime ¥

BEFORE YOU GET STARTED: READ THIS !

NOTES ON THE RECIPES

Follow one set of measurements

1 teaspoon = 5 ml
1 tablespoon = 15 ml
1 cup = 250 ml

Use fresh ingredients, including herbs

Wash ingredients, if appropriate, before preparing

Use ordinary fine salt unless sea salt flakes are specified

Use whichever type of butter you prefer

All the recipes use Japanese rice

Use medium eggs, unless otherwise specified

A NOTE ON THE CHAPTERS

Rather than organise this cookbook in the traditional Breakfast, Lunch and Dinner chapters, it has been designed to take you on a tour of every level of Tokyo gastronomy from the ground up (actually, from the underground up). If you're new to Japanese cuisine, start by reading about basic ingredients in the *Depachika* chapter on page 14, based on department store basement food halls. Next, we move on to 'B1F', street level, where we visit the greatest hits of subway station kiosks, convenience stores and vending machines. '1F' (the ground floor to Brits) features the recipes that are traditional to Tokyo - think soba, ramen and sushi. Up the elevator to '2F', and we're feasting on Japanese regional cuisine, including dishes from Hokkaido, Okinawa, Osaka and more. Foreign-influenced food has a huge influence on Tokyo cuisine, so '3F' is a celebration of all these crazy delicious hybrids: things like poke, pizza, pasta and choux buns, all with a distinctly Japanese twist. As many Tokyoites live in apartments, '4F' is dedicated to the best home-cooked meals around, including bento, breakfast, stir-fries, and anything that can be whipped up in a small kitchen. Finally, we finish on the rooftop bar, '5F', modern Tokyo fusion foods, with a couple of cocktails to finish it all off.

Cook from it however you like - most dishes are full meals on their own, but some are smaller, so they're best served with other dishes, or just a bowl of rice and miso soup. You can start with the simpler recipes found in found Tokyo Street on page 30, or At Home In Tokyo on page 180, or just dive in to the deep end - everything is achievable!

A NOTE ON DEEP-FRYING

When deep-frying, use a very large, deep pan. The surface of the oil should be at least 10 cm (4 in) below the rim of the pan to avoid overflow. Use a neutral oil with a high smoke point, such as groundnut (peanut), sunflower or rapeseed (canola) oil, and use a probe thermometer to check oil temperatures - they are available online or at kitchen supply shops.

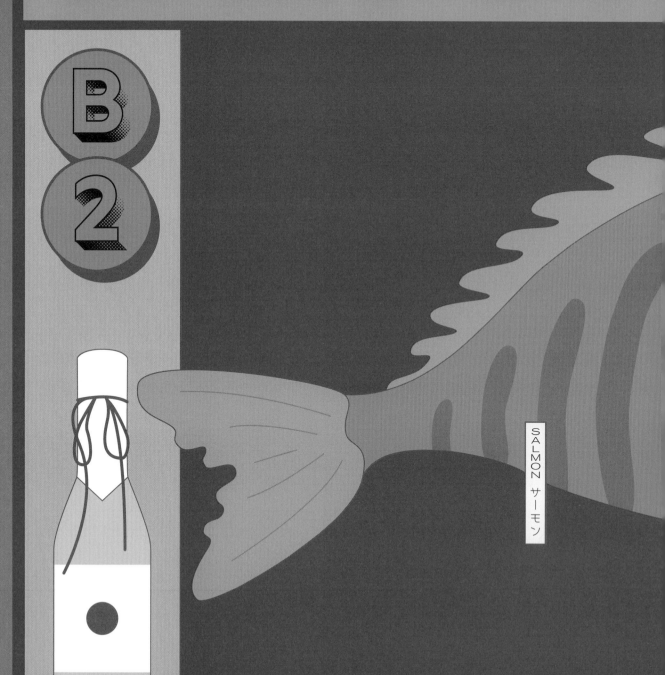

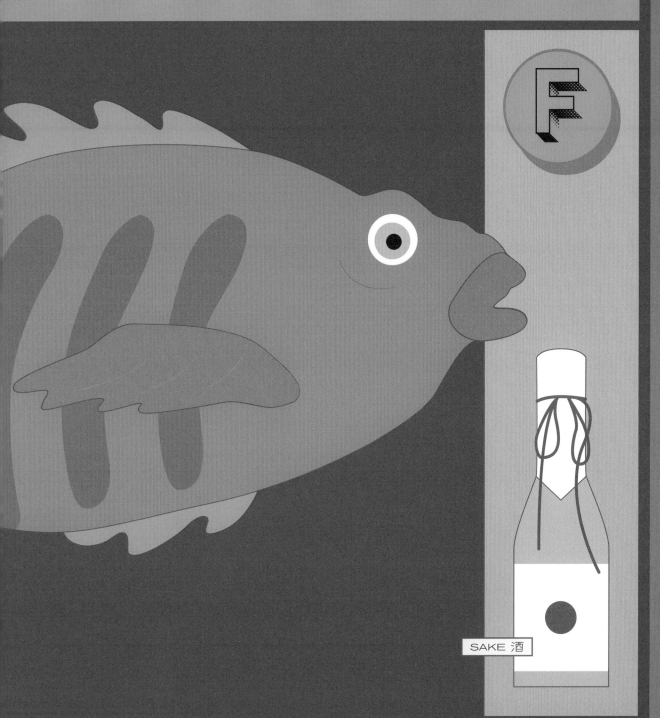

B2F

DEPACHIKA

DEPACHIKA

DEPACHIKA

A GUIDE TO JAPANESE INGREDIENTS

If you've only got a day or two to spend in Tokyo and you're looking for a good way to take in the city's food culture efficiently, an excellent microcosm would be one of Tokyo's many *depachika* - department store basement food halls. Sometimes, depachika are little more than very nice supermarkets, but more often they're sprawling vaults filled with highly specialised food and drink that can include beautiful bread and pâtisserie, fine cheeses, freshly made sushi, whole libraries of sake and wine, all sorts of bento, superlative seasonings, delicate traditional confections, and of course, some of the most gorgeous fresh produce on the planet, including the world-famous melons and mangoes sold as gifts that command more than ¥10,000 a pop.

I often spend hours perusing depachika - whenever I travel to Tokyo I always take an empty suitcase along to stock up on stuff to take home, and after a few trips to the food halls, that suitcase will inevitably be full to bursting. (As an aside, there are some restrictions on what you can take home, so check your local customs and excise site before shopping.) Depachika are so full of fascinating food they're almost like food museums - quite a bit of spectacle and showmanship, but also a good place to educate yourself on the enormous diversity of Tokyo's (and Japan's) gastronomy - starting with some basics.

MISO

Miso is one of my all-time favourite flavours – a combination of salty, sweet, tangy and umami, with complex aromas that can be fruity and light like fresh cheese, or bold and rich like balsamic vinegar. It's one of the best weapons to have in your culinary artillery, delivering a huge hit of moreish flavour to all kinds of cooking – not just Japanese. But, of course, it is a key component in a multitude of traditional and modern Japanese dishes, and its funky fermented aroma (characteristic of products made with *koji* mould, Japan's national fungus) is unmistakably Japanese. Start with a basic white miso and a basic red miso to familiarise yourself with their flavours, then explore the outer limits of the miso galaxy and take your cooking into new frontiers of flavour.

SOY SAUCE

Soy sauce is one of the flavours most associated with Japanese food, and I think one of the flavours that makes it so popular. It's salty-malty, Bovril-beefy, deeply umami and slightly tangy, which is what makes it easy to love (have you ever heard anyone say that soy sauce was an acquired taste for them?) and easy to cook with. At a depachika – or any Japanese supermarket – you'll find dozens of varieties ranging from thick and rich tamari to light, wheat-based *shiro shoyu* ('white' soy sauce) as well as obscure soy sauces like unpasteurised 'raw' soy sauce or soy sauces brewed with sea vegetables or sea animals for extra depth and umami, a bit like fish sauce. But you should start with a *koikuchi* soy sauce, which actually means 'rich,' but it's the basic, go-to variety that works in most dishes or as a condiment. Get a good-quality one made from just wheat, soybeans, salt, and water, and make sure you get a Japanese one – the Chinese ones aren't all bad or anything, but they do taste different. If you like you can also get an *usukuchi* (weak) soy sauce, which is good if you want a lighter flavour – especially useful for tofu, seasoning dashi or broths without overpowering them, or for mild-flavoured white fish.

TSUKEMONO

Japanese pickles, *tsukemono*, are also likely to catch your eye – and your nose – while wandering through a depachika. All manner of tasty plants are preserved in all manner of ways, like daikon buried in rice bran, a mélange of root veg cooked in a sweet-and-sour syrup (page 103), spicy salted mustard greens, punchy lacto-soured plums, or cucumbers simply brined until tart and refreshing. These are often displayed in their pickling medium in big crates or barrels, and if it weren't for the smell (which can range from a light vinegar aroma to full-on earthy stank) it would almost look like a kind of vegetable candy shop, full of vibrant pinks and purples and greens and yellows – the aubergines (eggplants) can even take on a bluish tinge. The flavours and textures of Japanese pickles are as wide-ranging as their appearance, and they're an easy way to introduce a distinctly Japanese flavour to a meal – a few of them alongside bowls of miso soup and rice with a simply cooked protein or vegetable dish is a classic Japanese dinner arrangement.

SAKE

Sake is usually called rice wine, but the way it's made is more like brewing beer – the starch in grains (in this case, rice) is converted into sugar (by our old friend koji mould – page 23) and then boiled, cooled, inoculated with yeast and fermented into alcohol. But it is wine-like in at least one sense, and that is its strength – sake is typically around 14–16% alcohol, not spirit-strength as many people think. It's a notable potable for many reasons, but particularly for its umami content and, in fact, sake is labelled with an amino acid score, which is meant to indicate how savoury it is. This makes it nice to drink, of course, but also excellent to cook with – it can add a strong yet subtle depth of flavour to dishes even in small quantities. I sometimes describe sake in cooking as a bit like soy sauce without the salt, which may be hard to get your head around, but it can deliver the same kind of malty, rich, slightly earthy flavour, and it has a little bit of sweetness and acidity, too.

There are many, many, many kinds of sake, but don't bother using anything too good for cooking – what you want is a nice, cheap plonk sake – it should be drinkable, but only just. There is also cooking sake, *ryorishu*, which is typically made from distilled alcohol combined with a fermented rice seasoning and other additives. Definitely not for drinking but most of this stuff is perfectly fine for cooking – just be wary of cooking sake that has added salt, because it can throw off your seasoning unpredictably.

節削り

物向け

300g	1,13
300g ビニールパック	1,1
500g	1,89
500g ビニールパック	1,9
1kg	3,78

MIRIN

Mirin is a kind of highly sweetened sake that delivers a similar malty rice flavour with extra sugar and viscosity. The top-quality stuff is called *hon mirin* (real mirin) and it is made purely through brewing, without any additions or subtractions along the way. Hon mirin can be really, really delicious, especially when it's made from brown rice, which gives it a slightly nutty, caramel-like flavour. But for most everyday cooking, you'll be fine using the not-as-nice but much cheaper 'mirin-style' seasoning, still made from fermented rice but with little or no alcohol, and padded with flavourings and syrups. Sure, it's not as good as the real stuff, but in many recipes, mirin is there mainly for sweetness and so mirin-style seasoning is fine.

RICE VINEGAR

Just like sake and mirin, the related rice vinegar comes in many grades and styles. Top-shelf rice vinegar is made just from soured fermented rice – which again, can be made from brown rice, or aged to produce really amazingly tasty vinegar. But a lot of rice vinegar is made partly or entirely from distilled vinegar, with koji rice flavourings added back in. And to be honest, most of this stuff is absolutely fine – it still doesn't have the harsh acidity of distilled vinegars or some of the hardcore rice vinegars from continental Asia. So like soy sauce, just make sure you get a Japanese rice vinegar; and like sake, be mindful that some cheaper rice vinegars contain salt.

DASHI AND TSUYU

Dashi is a broth made from infusing *kombu* (kelp) and *katsuobushi* (preserved smoked tuna shavings) into warm water, and it contributes one of two main Japanese flavour foundations in Japanese cooking (the other is koji). It's light yet meaty and satisfying, smoky and fishy and briny but in a subtle way that plays well with other flavours. Dashi can easily be made from scratch (page 184) but is even more easily – and more commonly – made from a powder or concentrate. Dashi powder is surprisingly refined stuff, with a full, satisfying, remarkably 'authentic' flavour, unlike that of the Western equivalent, the stock cube. For most home cooks, dashi powder is a storecupboard staple – great for making dashi, of course, but also a fantastic seasoning, a trick I learned from my mother-in-law. Sprinkle some into your fried rice or put some in a pasta sauce – it adds a wonderful rich flavour in the same way anchovies do, but without so much salt.

Similar convenience products are bottled liquid dashi, dashi concentrates, or *tsuyu*. These are often naturally brewed and taste more like 'real' dashi – I guess because that's what they are! Tsuyu is dashi that has already been concentrated and seasoned with things like soy sauce, sake, mirin or sugar, so it's ready to go as a dip, or can be diluted with water to make broths or bases for other dishes. Tsuyu is really delicious, with a synergistic umami effect from the combination of kombu, katsuobushi and soy sauce.

KOJI

Koji is the Japanese vernacular word for *Aspergillus oryzae*, a strain of mould used to saccharify and ferment grains and pulses in the production of soy sauce, miso, sake, rice vinegar and dozens of other essential Japanese products. As it ferments it leaves behind a distinctive earthy-fruity aroma that is considered one of the foundations of Japanese flavour (along with dashi), and it is so important in traditional Japanese gastronomy that it has been named the 'national fungus' of Japan.

デパ地下

24

NOODLES

Noodles come in many forms in Japan: instant, dried, fresh or frozen. Some, like soba or somen, are good dried and are actually rarely sold fresh, but others really are best if they're fresh or frozen. Ramen and udon, in particular, I feel are really only worth eating when they're fresh, because so much of their texture is lost when they're dried. However, I will say instant noodles are often surprisingly good, as the flash-frying method used to process them seems to retain their structure a bit better.

CITRUS

Japan has some of the most amazing fruit I've ever seen, but I always make a beeline for the citrus section in depachika. Some of them are just great to eat on their own, like super-sweet *dekopon* tangerines, or the mandarin-pomelo hybrid called *ponkan*, but others are wonderful for cooking. *Yuzu*, with its incomparable evergreen/lemon-lime aroma, is a classic, but also look out for lime-like varieties like *sudachi* or *kabosu*, powerful enough to lift a bowl of soup or accent a piece of sushi with just a tiny slice.

FISH

Want tasty sashimi, but don't have the money? Pick up some fish from a depachika. You can get some really great-quality seafood, neatly cleaned and trimmed and packaged so all you have to do is take it home, slice it and garnish it. It's still not super-cheap but it's easily the most economical way to get your raw fish fix.

MUSHROOMS

Mushrooms are also enormously important in Japanese cookery, especially *shiitake*, with their wonderfully meaty flavour and texture. Then there's the spindly *enoki*, feathery *maitake*, juicy *eringi*, cute little *shimeji*, and rare varieties like *matsutake*, prized for their potent woody-spicy aroma and sold for up to ¥100,000 per kilo. Japanese mushrooms tend to be quite flavourful in general, and are delicious simply grilled with sea salt, or tempura-fried, or perhaps bathed in a simmering hotpot. But they're also great in stir-fries, soups and rice-based dishes.

ROOT VEGETABLES

It's widely noted that Japanese cooking is veg-heavy. I don't know if it actually deserves this reputation, especially compared to, say, Indian cooking, but the fact remains that the Japanese culinary tradition features innumerable ways of making delicious dishes out of boring vegetables. Root veg in particular – things like daikon, turnips, taro, burdock and carrots – seem to turn up in Japanese cookery a lot, I think because they're such good flavour sponges. A wedge of daikon cooked in a delicious dashi or sweet soy sauce will absorb that flavour thoroughly, releasing it onto the palate like a burst dam when crushed between the teeth. They also make fantastic crunchy pickles.

SEAWEED

Japan's mountainous terrain makes it difficult to farm but, luckily, the Japanese have always made the most of the bounty of sea vegetables that surround the archipelago. The most common seaweeds you'll need for Japanese cooking are kombu, nori and wakame. Kombu is dried kelp, which is used to make dashi, but also eaten once cooked until tender. Nori is sold in sheets, to be wrapped around sushi, or as little green flakes that are used as an aromatic and savoury garnish. Wakame is most famous for its inclusion in miso soup and salads, with a tender texture and iron-rich flavour. Start with these and then see what else you can find – there are amazing flavours to be found among the greens of the sea.

NON-JAPANESE STUFF

Japanese cuisine has by this point incorporated so much from around the world that I think it's fair to include some non-Japanese ingredients in a typical Japanese larder. For example, depachika will always have a good bakery, they'll have a reasonably good range of European cheeses, a solid selection of herbs and spices and, of course, a variety of key ingredients from Japan's neighbours, such as Sichuan chilli bean paste, Thai fish sauce or Korean kimchi. You wouldn't really need them if you're planning to cook strictly traditional Japanese food – but not a lot of people in Tokyo actually do that, and neither should you!

JAPANESE RICE

Often, a Japanese meal just isn't a Japanese meal without rice. And even if you're just passing through Tokyo on a stopover, you're likely to eat some rice. Japanese airlines typically serve it as part of their in-flight meals, and *onigiri* – seasoned rice balls – are one of the few snacks you'll be able to get in the surprisingly poorly serviced terminals of Narita Airport. You'll find it at every level of Japanese dining, in convenience stores, canteens, kiosks and curry houses, in home kitchens, izakaya and, of course, sushi bars. Even noodle shops often offer rice as a side dish, just in case the noodles themselves don't quite cut it. Which seems like a bit of an insult to noodles, but of course they are and forever will be just a pretender to the throne of Japanese Carb Emperor.

So, if you're going to cook Japanese food at home, you gotta cook Japanese rice. And it's not hard, but it isn't quite as simple as throwing it in a pan with some water and boiling it. Japanese rice cooks by absorption, which means you'll need to be a little more precise with it, and you'll need firstly a pan with a snug-fitting lid and secondly a reliable, adjustable heat source.

I always measure out rice by weight, which is easier and more accurate than by volume; you can simply weigh out everything into the pan you're cooking with, rather than dealing with cups or jugs. The ratio of rice to water is 1 to 1.3 by weight (which is about the same as 1 to 1.1 by volume, for reference), so, for example:

**for 300 g (10½ oz/1½ cups) rice
(enough for 4 servings)
you'd need 390 g
(13½ oz/scant 2 cups) of water**

Don't cook less than 150 g (5 oz/¼ cup) at a time because it's simply too little – the water will evaporate too quickly and most of the rice will end up stuck to the bottom of the pan.

But before you start the cooking, you need to do the washing. Weigh out your rice, then fill the pan with water and swish and massage the grains with your hand. Discard the water and repeat 3 or 4 times until the water is clear. A good rule of thumb I use to judge if the water is clear enough is when you can see individual grains of rice instead of a blurry, white cloud when it's covered with about 2 cm (¾ in) of water. Drain the rice well (use a sieve), then return the rice to the pan and cover with the measured amount of water. Leave to soak for at least half an hour, or an hour if you have time, then bring to a gentle boil. Place a lid on the pan, reduce the heat to low and set a timer for 15 minutes. When the time is up, kill the heat, then let the rice rest, covered, for at least 5 minutes, then remove the lid and enjoy.

BE SERIOUS ABOUT B. CEREUS – BUT DON'T BE SCARED OF LEFTOVER RICE

I hear a lot of people say they've always been taught you should never reheat rice. I don't know where this widespread misconception comes from, but it isn't true. Reheating rice isn't the problem – it's storing it at the wrong temperature. See, there's a nasty bug called *Bacillus cereus* that is sometimes present in rice grains, and it forms protective endospores that can survive cooking and then go on to germinate at temperatures between 10–50°C (50–120°F). So rice kept piping hot in a rice cooker will be fine, and so will rice that is cooled quickly – but if rice hangs around too long at room temperature it can create a risk of *B. cereus* growth and toxin production, neither of which will be removed by further cooking. So it's not about reheating – it's about cooling. Provided your rice has chilled down rapidly (within 2 hours), it will be absolutely fine to eat, either as is or reheated. To do this, simply leave your rice uncovered in a shallow container, not piled up too deep – if you have space in the freezer it should take less than half an hour to chill it down, or less than an hour in the fridge.

デパ地下

KEEPING JAPANESE RICE SOFT IN THE FRIDGE: A BASIC SOLUTION

27

Of course, this method of cooking rice is all well and good if you're planning to eat your rice right then and there – but as you probably already know, rice tends to go hard and dry in the fridge. This dried-out, crumbly rice is fantastic for fried rice, it freezes well (especially convenient if you bag it up in individual portions), and it can be easily microwaved back to life. But what if you want to make rice to have in a bento or as onigiri, which has to be refrigerated but won't be reheated?

Here's where you have to alter the chemical structure of your rice – it isn't as complicated or as scary as it sounds. For reasons I don't quite understand, rice goes hard because of how its starches behave during cooking and cooling, so the way to create rice that stays soft in the fridge is to mess with those starches. In commercial kitchens in Japan, they use a special enzyme blend for this, and while you can get it in the UK, it's hard to find and very expensive; you have to buy it in bulk, so it's not worth it unless you plan on making a hell of a lot of onigiri. But I've discovered a makeshift method to achieve soft cold rice at home: soak the rice with bicarbonate of soda (baking soda).

Fans of ramen and pretzels may already know that alkalinity does odd things to starches – making some more tender and others more resilient, and expediting browning as well. I'd read about treating rice with an alkaline solution to improve its texture, and while I don't think it works for hot, fresh rice, it works an absolute charm for cold rice. As I said, I don't really understand why – but it does. To me the result almost seems like rice that's too soft when it's fresh, but then it somehow tightens up to become the perfect texture after cooling. Honestly, I was amazed by how well this worked.

THIS IS THE RECIPE FOR 300 G (10½ OZ/ 1½ CUPS) OF RICE, WHICH IS ENOUGH FOR ABOUT 3-4 BENTO OR 5-6 ONIGIRI

300 g (10½ oz/1½ cups) Japanese rice
3 g (½ teaspoon) bicarbonate of soda (baking soda)
300 ml (10 fl oz/1¼ cups) water, plus 390 ml (13¾ fl oz/1½ cups)

METHOD
Combine the rice, bicarbonate of soda and 300 ml (10 fl oz/1¼ cups) of water in a saucepan and stir it around to dissolve the bicarbonate of soda. Leave to soak for 1½ hours, then discard the water and wash the rice well. Cover the rice with the 390 ml (13¾ fl oz/ 1½ cups) of water and bring to the boil, then place a lid on the pan and reduce the heat to low. Cook, covered, for 13 minutes (the bicarbonate of soda will make the rice absorb the water more quickly), then immediately uncover; the rice should appear overcooked, so don't be alarmed if it looks mushy and wrong. Tip the rice onto a tray or plate to cool. When the rice reaches room temperature, toss the grains with chopsticks to break them up, refrigerate uncovered until totally chilled, then cover and consume within 4 days.

Note that this method will turn the rice pale yellow, which is weird but harmless, and it may also have a faintly soapy flavour – but this will not be noticeable when paired with the strong-flavoured ingredients you'd typically find in bento or onigiri. This rice will be supple and delicious straight from the fridge, but it will be a little better if you give it half an hour to an hour to come up to room temperature.

デパ地下

TOKYO

MOMO 桃

STREET

ICHIGO SANDO いちごサンド

F

MOMOTARO 桃太郎

B
1
F

TOKYO STREET

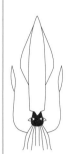

TOKYO STREET

TOKYO STREET

SUBWAY STATION KIOSKS, CONVENIENCE STORES AND VENDING MACHINES

Tokyo is filled with things to amaze and impress, but it's the little things that make daily life there so bearable compared to similarly huge, stressful cites. For example, one of my favourite Tokyo minutiae is the pleasant melodies that play when train doors are closing (so much nicer than the *completely* unnecessary honking beeps you hear on the London Underground). And then there's the convenience food - snacks and sweets or full meals you can purchase from vending machines, 7-Elevens or little stands set up in stations or streets. In most countries, this kind of grab-and-go food would be terrible to mediocre, but in Japan it's actually really good. This is because of distribution systems that allow for multiple deliveries of fresh food throughout the day, and because of a national ethos of attention to detail combined with enthusiastic adoption of cutting-edge food technology. Seriously, you can eat very well in Tokyo even if you just ate at Lawsons, Family Marts and Mini Stops. Sure, you'd be missing out, but I'd also argue you'd be missing out if you *didn't* eat from conbini, at least a few times. They really are fantastic!

CORN POTAGE

One of the greatest things about vending machines in Japan is that they dispense hot drinks as well as cold ones – tea and coffee, of course, but also creamy soups, especially the ubiquitous corn potage. Simple and sweet, this winter staple comes in a hot steel can that warms your hands before it warms your gullet. On a cold, drizzly day (all too common in Tokyo), there's almost nothing I'd rather drink.

34

SERVES 4

25 g (1 oz) butter
¼ onion, finely diced
pinch of salt
pinch of pepper (white pepper, ideally)
360–400 g (12–14 oz/large) tin of creamed corn
200 ml (7 fl oz/scant 1 cup) milk
200 ml (7 fl oz/scant 1 cup) single (light) cream
150–200 g (5–7 oz/small) tin of sweetcorn, drained,
    or the kernels from 1 ear of fresh corn
pinch of MSG or chicken stock powder (optional)

METHOD

Melt the butter in a deep saucepan and add the onion, salt and pepper. Cook gently over a medium-low heat until the onions soften and turn translucent (try not to let them brown very much). Add the creamed corn, milk and cream, bring to the boil, then simmer for 5 minutes. Purée until very smooth in a blender or with a hand-held blender. Return to the pan and add the corn and the MSG or chicken stock powder, if using. Bring back to the boil, taste and adjust the seasoning as necessary. Serve in mugs or cups so you can feel the warmth of the soup in your hands as you drink it ... ahhhhh.

東京ストリート

AFTERNOON MILK TEA

'AFTERNOON TEA HAS BEEN DRUNK BY THE ENGLISH EVER SINCE THE CUSTOM WAS FIRST STARTED BY THE DUCHESS OF BEDFORD IN THE MID 19TH CENTURY.'

So explains the label on a bottle of *Gogo no Kocha* ('Afternoon Tea'), one of the more ubiquitous black tea brands in Japan. When I first encountered this stuff, which was actually back in LA's Little Tokyo rather than Big Tokyo, I thought it was delightfully weird for a number of reasons, primarily because I'd never had milky tea before (it would be another five years or so before I moved to the UK) and because I thought the English noblewoman depicted on the label was Queen Elizabeth, which would have been a bold and probably illegal usage of her likeness. Of course, I now realise it must be the Duchess of Bedford, and I guess we have her to thank for this lovely concoction of highly sweetened, very milky tea. For me it's actually a bit rich for daily drinking – I tend to prefer the more bracing, refreshing bottled green teas – but it was always a lovely afternoon treat, almost like a tea-flavoured milkshake. That's because I believe it's made by infusing the tea directly into milk, rather than just adding a splash of milk to tea brewed in water – so it's super-milky and rich.

MAKES 1 LITRE (34 FL OZ/4 CUPS) OF TEA

1 litre (34 fl oz/4 cups) whole milk
4 black tea bags
4–6 tablespoons golden caster (superfine) sugar

METHOD

Place 250 ml (8½ fl oz/1 cup) of the milk in a saucepan along with the tea bags and sugar. Bring to a simmer, stir to dissolve the sugar, then remove from the heat and add the remaining milk. Transfer to the fridge and leave to infuse for 2 hours. Remove the tea bags. Keep in bottles in the fridge for up to 3 days and serve well chilled.

東京ストリート

ROASTED GRAIN TEA

MUGICHA

Japanese vending machines are chock-full of delicious teas, always available cold but also sometimes hot, in special insulated bottles. Most of these are varieties of green tea, but some of my favourites are based on hearty roasted grains like barley, buckwheat, brown rice, or Job's-tears, a type of millet with a rich, nutty flavour. They're still very refreshing, and they're caffeine-free – which is nice, because in Japan I got addicted to caffeine as I just wasn't paying attention to how much I was consuming. With delicious bottled tea and coffee at every turn, it's easy to go overboard.

To recreate that vending-machine convenience at home, I simply brew this in a big batch, bottle it, and keep it in the fridge for whenever I need some healthy refreshment.

MAKES ABOUT 2 LITRES (70 FL OZ/8 CUPS)
OF TEA

25 g (1 oz/2 tablespoons) pearl barley
50 g (2 oz/¼ cup) other whole grains (I like a mixture of buckwheat and spelt, but other options are brown rice, farro or rye)
2 litres (70 fl oz/8 cups) water

METHOD

Put the grains in a dry frying pan (skillet) and set over a medium heat. Cook the grains, stirring frequently, until they are deep brown and smell very toasty (take them very far, until they begin to smell burnt). Remove from the pan and leave to cool. Keep in an airtight container until ready to use.

To make a big batch of tea, place all the roasted grains in a saucepan with the water and bring to the boil. Remove from the heat and leave to infuse for 10 minutes. Pass through a sieve and drink hot, or cool completely, then transfer to bottles or jars and keep in the fridge.

To make individual cups, place 1 tablespoon of the toasted grains in a teapot and pour over 200 ml (7 fl oz/scant 1 cup) of boiling water. Infuse for 5 minutes, then strain and enjoy.

東京ストリート

CALPIS SODA

40

Calpis is perhaps best known outside Japan for its somewhat off-putting name (see also: Pocari Sweat), and it doesn't sound that much better when you describe what it actually is: a carbonated yoghurt drink. The literal meaning of the name doesn't particularly help, either – a portmanteau of 'calcium' and the sanskrit *sarpis*: butter flavour. (Mmmmm, buttery calcium.) But it usually only takes one sip to overcome all of this, because it's so very delicious. The yoghurt flavour is simply a light and refreshing tang – nothing cheesy or sour that you might expect from a fizzy dairy product. Almost every vending machine in Japan will serve some variation of it, but making it at home is nearly as easy as buying it pre-made, and it uses very common ingredients.

MAKES ENOUGH CONCENTRATE
FOR 10-12 GLASSES OF CALPIS

6 tablespoons lemon juice
200 g (7 oz/scant 1 cup) golden caster
    (superfine) sugar
300 g (10½ oz/1¼ cups) plain yoghurt
sparkling water

METHOD

Whisk together the lemon juice, sugar and yoghurt until the sugar dissolves. Pass through a fine sieve, then keep in the fridge for up to a week.

To make a glass of calpis, combine one part of the yoghurt mixture with three parts sparkling water. It is best served over ice.

東京ストリート

IN KABUKICHO
TO THE KARAOKE BOX!
WHERE BEERS ARE PRICY

SO FIRST: TO THE CONBINI
TO FILL OUR BAGS WITH TINS:
HIGHBALLS AND KIRIN

UNDER THE TABLE
WE FILL OUR GLASSES!

STRONG AND DRY LEMON CHU-HAI

SHOCHU HIGHBALL

Japanese vending machines aren't just for soft stuff – many boast a delightful array of things to get you blotto, including god-awful beer, surprisingly excellent beer, 'one cup' servings of sake and little bottles of whisky (sometimes really good whisky). But my favourite vending machine booze is the glorious *chu-hai*, short for shochu highball. Chu-hai are Japan's answer to alcopops, usually between 4% and 8% alcohol, almost always fruit-flavoured but rarely sickly sweet like fizzy drinks. My favourite tinned chu-hai are strong and bone-dry, made with a generous measure of shochu, little or no sugar, and a sharp citrus element like yuzu or grapefruit. Probably the most basic, no-frills, entry-level tinned chu-hai is the lemon-flavoured stuff, which is still one of my favourites. It's stark and austere, but it's also a kind of lemonade for grown-ups – fizzy, fun and a highly effective attitude adjuster.

By the way, 75 ml (2½ fl oz/scant ⅓ cup) may sound like a lot of booze, but bear in mind shochu is typically only 25% alcohol, so the finished drink will be about 7–8%.

MAKES 1 HIGHBALL

75 ml (2½ fl oz/scant ⅓ cup) shochu
¼ lemon
1 teaspoon caster (superfine) sugar (or more or less, to taste)
ice cubes
150–175 ml (5–6 fl oz/about ¾ cup) sparkling water

METHOD

Combine the shochu, lemon and sugar in a highball glass and muddle together until the sugar dissolves. Add the ice cubes, then top up with the sparkling water. Stir well and enjoy.

ONIGIRI

FILLED RICE BALLS

46

Onigiri are a bit like the traditional Japanese answer to sandwiches – starchy thing filled with flavourful thing – and the same kind of light lunch/convenient and transportable tummy-fillers. Onigiri also compete with sandwiches to be the largest occupier of conbini shelf space – most branches will have dozens of varieties, filled with all sorts of delightful things. And one of the coolest things about onigiri is how they're packaged – they come in these ingenious plastic sleeves that keep the nori separated from the rice until they're unwrapped, so it stays nice and crisp. Onigiri can be stuffed with almost anything (tuna mayo is a popular option for the less adventurous; *mentaiko*, spicy fish roe, is one for the sensation seekers), but I think the best fillings are the ones with a lot of flavour to season the rice – here are a few of my favourites. Kewpie mayo, by the way, is a Japanese brand of mayo with a bit more seasoning than standard Western brands. If you can't find it, you can approximate the flavour by mixing ¼ teaspoon of dashi powder, ¼ teaspoon of Dijon mustard and some salt and finely ground white pepper into 100 g (3½ oz) of your regular mayonnaise.

If you're making onigiri to have fresh, use the instructions to cook Japanese rice (page 26). If you're planning to keep them in the fridge to eat later, use the instructions for rice that will stay soft (page 27). You'll need 60 g (2 oz/⅓ cup) of uncooked Japanese rice and half a sheet of nori for each onigiri.

To assemble, dip your hands in lightly salted water and grab a handful of rice. Flatten the rice out into a round using your palms, and place a spoonful of filling in the centre, then gather up the edges to form a ball. Press each ball into a triangle shape using the inside of the joint between your thumb and index finger as a guide (this will take practise, but once you get the hang of it, it's quite fun). Wrap in nori just before tucking in.

UMEBOSHI AND KATSUOBUSHI

PICKLED PLUM AND SMOKED TUNA

3 tablespoons rehydrated katsuobushi (from making Dashi, page 184)
6 *umeboshi*, stones removed

Squeeze any excess water out of the katsuobushi. Roughly chop the umeboshi and katsuobushi together to form a chunky paste.

WAKAME AND TOASTED SESAME

WAKAME SEAWEED AND TOASTED SESAME

3 tablespoons dried wakame
2 tablespoons white sesame seeds, toasted until deep golden brown
pinch of salt

Rehydrate the wakame in warm water for about 30 minutes, then squeeze dry and finely chop. Fold the wakame, sesame and salt into the cooked rice while it's still warm, then shape into onigiri.

EBI MAYO

PRAWN MAYO

6 prawns (shrimp), shelled, deveined and cooked
50 g (2 oz/scant ¼ cup) Kewpie mayo (see opposite)
pinch of *shichimi* (optional)
pinch of dashi powder (optional)

Coarsely chop the prawns and stir them together with the mayo and the shichimi and dashi powders, if using. Leave to mingle in the fridge for an hour, if you have the time, so the prawn flavour starts to permeate the mayo.

東京ストリート

ODEN

HEARTY DASHI SOUP

There's nothing like sticking your face in a cloud of *oden* steam on a winter's day – it's the gastronomic equivalent of a dip in a hot spring bath. Oden is one of Japan's most cheap-and-cheerful hotpot dishes, which can easily be made at home but even more easily purchased from a dedicated shop or convenience store. Essentially, it's a bunch of stuff cooked in a slightly sweetened, light yet fortifying dashi, and that stuff can be almost anything as long as it's cheap and soaks up the liquid nicely. This means you'll always find fish cakes, tofu (especially fried), minced (ground) meat or cuts suitable to braising, and firm yet porous vegetables like potatoes, cabbage and daikon. Shops that sell oden have everything hot-held in barely simmering broth, so whatever they sell has to have the structural integrity to hold together after a long soak. The way it works is you choose what size portion you want, then you choose the items you like, typically sold on sticks for ease of eating. It's always unbelievably good value, because the ingredients are humble and the volume is enormous.

SERVES 4-6

For the dashi

2 litres (70 fl oz/8 cups) dashi
60 ml (2 fl oz/¼ cup) soy sauce
4 tablespoons sake
2 tablespoons golden caster (superfine) sugar
½ teaspoon salt

For the oden

8 cabbage leaves
300 g (10½ oz) minced (ground) chicken
1 garlic clove, very finely chopped
¼ onion, finely chopped or grated
1 spring onion (scallion), finely sliced
1 teaspoon sake
½ teaspoon soy sauce
pinch of salt
8 small or 4 large octopus legs
400 g (14 oz) konnyaku noodles
4 pieces (80–100 g/3–3½ oz) abura-age, cut into
    triangles
4 eggs, soft-boiled and peeled
300 g (10½ oz) chikuwa, or similar fish-cake product
    such as hanpen or satsuma-age
300 g (10½ oz) firm, waxy potatoes, peeled
½ large daikon, peeled and cut into
    2.5-cm (1-in) thick rounds
hot mustard, to serve

METHOD

Combine the dashi, soy sauce, sake, sugar and salt in a large pan and bring to a low boil. Add the cabbage leaves and cook until soft and pliable, about 5 minutes, then remove from the liquid and cool.

Combine the chicken, garlic, onion, spring onion, sake, soy sauce and salt, and mix well, then divide into 8 oblong meatballs. Wrap the chicken balls up in the cabbage leaves using a burrito-like 'roll-and-tuck' method, folding the sides up around the filling before rolling it up. Secure each roll with a cocktail stick (toothpick) or skewer. Return the dashi to the boil and blanch the octopus legs in the dashi for about 5 minutes, or until firm. Thread each one onto a skewer.

Now, simply cook everything in the dashi to your liking – it's best to do this low and slow, with the liquid barely simmering, so the ingredients have plenty of time to soak up the delicious dashi. Start with the octopus, as they will need at least an hour to soften, and they will provide a lovely flavour to the broth. Everything else can be added whenever, and removed and eaten when it's ready – the ideal way to eat oden is gathered around a table with a gas burner. Put a little mustard in side dishes for people to season their oden as they like. This is wonderful with hot sake or shochu.

東京ストリート

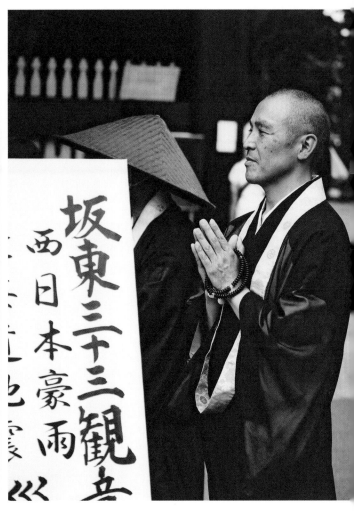

50

NIKUMAN

STEAMED MEAT DUMPLINGS

Japanese convenience stores have mastered the modern art of hot-holding. Teas and coffees, piping hot but not so hot they burn your mouth; fried chicken, basking in ventilated warming cupboards so they stay crisp and juicy; and the king of hot, steamy instant gratification: *nikuman*.

Nikuman are Japanese steamed meat dumplings, ancestors of fluffy steamed Chinese dumplings such as *char siu bao*. Japanese versions tend to be bigger than the Chinese originals – more like the size of a little burger rather than a dinner roll – and less sweet. They are juicy and steamy and satisfying, perhaps the greatest grab-and-go food item in the world.

MAKES 6 BIG OR 8 SMALL NIKUMAN

For the nikuman dough
100 ml (3½ fl oz/scant ½ cup) warm water
7 g (2 teaspoons) dried yeast
200 g (7 oz/scant 1⅔ cups) plain (all-purpose) flour, plus extra for dusting
2 tablespoons caster (superfine) sugar
1 teaspoon baking powder
1 teaspoon sesame oil
1 teaspoon vegetable oil

For the pork filling
250 g (9 oz) well-fatted minced (ground) pork
50 g (2 oz) bamboo shoots, finely diced
2 dried shiitake mushrooms, rehydrated, destemmed and finely diced
3 stalks of nira, coarsely chopped
125 g (4 oz) piece of ginger root, peeled and grated
1 tablespoon soy sauce
1 tablespoon oyster sauce
1 tablespoon cornflour (cornstarch)
1 teaspoon sesame oil
¼ teaspoon salt
¼ teaspoon white pepper

METHOD

For the dough, combine the warm water with the yeast and stir to dissolve. Stir together the flour, sugar and baking powder in a bowl, then add the liquid ingredients and mix to combine. Use a stand mixer with a dough hook to knead the dough for 10 minutes, or knead by hand for 15 minutes, until the dough is smooth and supple. Cover the dough loosely with cling film (plastic wrap) and leave to prove for about an hour until it roughly doubles in size.

Meanwhile, combine all the filling ingredients in a bowl and mix well.

Punch down the dough and divide it into 6 or 8 equal-sized balls. Roll out the balls on a lightly floured surface into rounds about 5 mm (¼ in) thick. Place a spoonful of filling in the centre of each round. Gather the dough around the filling, and pinch to seal.

Line a steamer with baking parchment (wooden steamers are best, as they conduct less heat and will create a softer dough) and place over boiling water. Steam smaller buns for 12 minutes and larger buns for 15 minutes. You can check that they are cooked through by inserting a thin knife or metal skewer into the centre of a bun. Hold it there for 30 seconds and if it comes out hot to the touch they're cooked through. These reheat nicely in the microwave, so don't worry about making too many. Besides, they will get eaten!

東京ストリート

PIZZAMAN

STEAMED PIZZA DUMPLINGS

53

Pizzaman: a superhero of conbini, here to save you from hunger (and often, from getting too drunk).

Apparently the Japanese are of the same mindset as the Americans when it comes to pizza, in the sense that they figure pizza is so delicious, everything should kind of be pizza. Case in point: pizzaman, a version of nikuman flavoured with ... pizza stuff – cheese, meat, tomatoes, etc. I mean honestly if you can't get behind a steamed dumpling filled with pizza toppings, then there is just no hope for you.

MAKES 6 BIG OR 8 SMALL PIZZAMAN

1 quantity Nikuman Dough (page 50)
1 tablespoon olive oil
100 g (3½ oz) minced (ground) pork or Italian
    sausage meat
50 g (2 oz) pepperoni
salt and freshly ground black pepper
50 g (2 oz) passata (sieved tomatoes)
20 g (¾ oz) Parmesan, grated
handful of basil leaves, torn (optional)
100 g (3½ oz) mozzarella
a little plain (all-purpose) flour, for dusting

METHOD

Heat the olive oil in a pan and sauté the pork or sausage and pepperoni until cooked through. Season with salt and pepper and add the passata. Continue to cook for about 30 minutes until much of the liquid has evaporated and the mixture is thick and rich. Remove from the heat and stir in the Parmesan and basil, if using. Leave to cool completely.

Punch down the nikuman dough and divide it into 6 or 8 equal-sized balls. Roll out the balls on a lightly floured surface into rounds about 5 mm (¼ in) thick. Place a spoonful of filling in the centre of each round, place chunk of mozzarella on top of the filling, then gather the dough around the filling and pinch to seal.

Line a steamer with baking parchment (wooden steamers are best, as they conduct less heat and will create a softer dough) and place over boiling water. Steam smaller buns for 10 minutes and larger buns for 12 minutes. If you want to check that they are hot throughout, insert a thin knife or skewer in the middle and hold for 30 seconds. If it comes out hot to the touch, the food is ready.

東
京
ス
ト
リ
ー
ト

CHEESE-STUFFED FRIED CHICKEN

54

While it doesn't quite compare to restaurants and street stalls that cook it to order, the fried chicken you can get at conbini is surprisingly good. Of course, that's partly due to the many novel variations in which it is available, such as buttered scallop flavour, yuzu chilli flavour, or even 'ramen' flavour. But my favourite is the cheese-stuffed fried chicken, an item so ridiculous it really could only be Japanese or American. In other words, exactly my kind of food. You will need a probe thermometer for this one.

MAKES 4 PIECES

4 boneless chicken thighs, skin on
80 g (3 oz) mild Cheddar, cut into 4 rectangles
1 egg
1 teaspoon soy sauce
100 g (3½ oz/heaped ¾ cup) plus 1 tablespoon
    cornflour (cornstarch)
50 g (2 oz/heaped ⅓ cup) plain (all-purpose) flour
¼ teaspoon salt
1 teaspoon black pepper
oil, for deep-frying
ketchup or chilli sauce, to serve

METHOD

Stuff a piece of cheese under the skin of each chicken thigh and weave a cocktail stick (toothpick) through the skin and meat to seal the cheese inside. Beat the egg and soy sauce together with 1 tablespoon of cornflour, then dip the chicken thighs in this mixture. Combine the remaining cornflour with the plain flour, salt and pepper and mix well. Dredge the chicken thighs in the seasoned flour, then leave them for about 10 minutes, so the flour hydrates and clings to the chicken.

Heat the oil to 170°C (340°F). Dredge the chicken in the flour mixture a second time, shaking off any excess. Fry for 6–8 minutes until the internal temperature is at least 75°C (170°F) and it is golden brown, then drain. Serve with ketchup and/or chilli sauce.

東
京
ス
ト
リ
ー
ト

TERIYAKI CHICKEN AND BOILED EGG SANDO

58

Although conbini sandwiches can be pretty bland and basic, there are a few that are genuinely exquisite, like this teriyaki chicken and boiled egg item, which was probably my favourite conbini sando when I lived in Japan, and maybe the only one I actually have cravings for from time to time. The chicken-and-egg combo is great by itself, by the way – instead of having it between two slices of bread, you could just have it with a bowl of rice and some salad for a lovely dinner.

MAKES 4 SANDOS

4 eggs
100 ml (3½ fl oz/scant ½ cup) soy sauce
100 ml (3½ fl oz/scant ½ cup) mirin
4 tablespoons sake
50 g (2 oz/¼ cup) light soft brown sugar
2 garlic cloves, grated
2 teaspoons cornflour (cornstarch) mixed with
    1 tablespoon cold water
4 boneless, skinless chicken thighs
8 slices of white bread
4 tablespoons Kewpie mayo (page 46)
a few lettuce leaves

METHOD

Boil the eggs perfectly. Easier said than done, right? What you want are eggs that are medium boiled – they need to be firm enough to slice, and the yolks should be mostly set, but still ever so slightly gooey in the centre. There are many variables at play in egg boiling, but as long as you control as many of them as possible, you should achieve egg nirvana. Here is what works for me: I keep my eggs in the fridge, I use medium eggs, and always start with water at a rolling boil. I lower the eggs into the water carefully with a slotted spoon, and cook them for 7½ minutes (this will be more like 7 minutes for small eggs or 8 minutes for large eggs). As soon as the time's up, I drain the eggs and chill them in cold water. Let them chill thoroughly, as this will make them easier to peel (old eggs, rather than fresh ones, are also easier to peel, by the way).

Combine the soy sauce, mirin, sake, brown sugar and garlic in a deep frying pan (skillet) and bring to the boil. Stir in the cornflour slurry to thicken, then add the chicken thighs. Cook in the sauce for about 10 minutes, basting continuously, until the chicken is cooked through and the sauce has reduced slightly and glazed the chicken nicely (keep the heat moderate so the sauce doesn't over-reduce). Remove from the heat and leave to cool.

Slice the chicken and the eggs. To assemble the sandwiches, spread one slice of bread with the mayo, then add the lettuce, then the sliced chicken, then a little more sauce, and finally the eggs and the other slice of bread. Like all conbini sandwiches, this will be good fresh but also equally good after a day in the fridge.

KATSU SANDO

FRIED PORK CHOP SANDWICH

60

While the quality of conbini food is generally great, and sometimes superb, one area where they disappoint is in the sandwich aisle. To be perfectly fair, conbini sandwiches are technically faultless – the conbini distribution model allows for multiple deliveries of freshly prepared food throughout the day, so you'll basically never find a conbini sandwich with soggy bread or wilted lettuce. But their actual contents are often the height of blandness – watery ham, iceberg lettuce, American cheese, tuna mayo, egg salad, etc., all invariably stuffed between slices of crustless and flavourless white bread (which I actually secretly love, but it's not exactly artisan sourdough).

But there is a conbini sandwich that is pretty much always delicious, and that's the *tonkatsu* sandwich, or *katsu sando*. That's deep-fried pork with tangy tonkatsu sauce, sometimes with mayo, egg, cabbage and other embellishments. And katsu sandos usually taste good even if their constituent parts aren't so good, mainly because tonkatsu sauce makes everything taste awesome, and because of the deep-fried pork. Hard to go wrong with deep-fried pork. Anyway, if bad katsu sandos are kind of okay, then imagine how good *good* katsu sandos are. And that's what this recipe is. It calls for a sprinkle of meat tenderiser powder, which I don't think is standard practice, but it helps make the meat easy to bite through, which is important to preserve the integrity of the sandwich.

Alternatively, you can just make the tonkatsu following the recipe on page 106, and then slap it between two slices of bread with sauce and mayo, and enjoy it while it's still hot and crisp – delicious.

You will need a probe thermometer for this one.

MAKES 4 SANDOS

4 pork loin cutlets/steaks, about 1 cm (½ in) thick
salt and white pepper
meat tenderiser powder
50 g (2 oz/heaped ⅓ cup) strong white bread flour
2 eggs, beaten with a splash of cold water
120 g (4 oz/2 cups) panko
oil, for deep-frying
8 slices soft yet sturdy white bread (cut the crusts off for an authentic conbini experience)
4 tablespoons Kewpie mayo (page 46)
½ hispi cabbage, finely shredded
100 ml (3½ fl oz/scant ½ cup) tonkatsu sauce

METHOD

Season the pork with salt and pepper and dust with a little meat tenderiser powder (use about as much as you would salt; too much will make the meat flabby, and too little will have no effect). Rub the seasonings into the meat and leave to sit in the fridge for at least an hour.

Heat the oil to 180°C (350°F). Dredge the pork in the flour, then the eggs, and then the panko, ensuring the cutlets are very well coated. Fry in the oil for 5–6 minutes, until the internal temperature of the pork 60°C (140°F) and it is golden brown – it's okay if it's still a little bit pink.

To construct the sandwich, spread the mayo on one piece of bread, then top with a handful of cabbage. Put a little tonkatsu sauce on top of the cabbage, then put the tonkatsu on top of that and add a little more tonkatsu sauce. Finally, top with the other piece of bread, squish it down, then slice in half. These are nice warm but they're also perfectly delicious cold, and their texture will be okay after 24 hours in the fridge, provided your bread isn't too dry and flimsy.

東京ストリート

STRAWBERRY SANDO

Of all the sandwiches to be found at a conbini, this one may be the most ridiculous. The strawberries and cream sandwich is a confusing thing to find in between the typical ham and tuna (is it ... savoury?), but it all makes perfect sense once you try it. Japanese white bread tends to be sweet and soft – and very bland – so when wrapped around strawberries and cream it simply becomes like a kind of cake. In fact, this looks an awful lot like a Victoria sponge, and it wouldn't be out of place in an afternoon tea (see also: Afternoon Milk Tea, page 37). If you have a fruit-sandwich craving (as we all do, of course) and strawberries aren't in season, this will work well with any fruit with a similar texture – kiwi, mango, pineapple and peaches are all delicious.

MAKES 4 HALF SANDOS

200 ml (7 fl oz/scant 1 cup) whipping cream
1 teaspoon vanilla extract
1 tablespoon caster (superfine) sugar
4 slices soft, sweet, white bread (or you can use
    brioche, which is delicious, but not typical),
    crusts removed
300 g (10½ oz) strawberries (about 18–20), halved

METHOD

Whip the cream with the vanilla and sugar to very stiff peaks – it should be a firm, spreadable consistency. Spread it evenly onto each slice of bread. Arrange the strawberries on 2 slices of the bread, then close the sandwiches. Wrap in cling film (plastic wrap) and refrigerate for 30–60 minutes, then unwrap and slice diagonally to serve.

東京ストリート

YAKISOBA AND YAKISOBA PAN

STIR-FRIED NOODLES AND STIR-FRIED NOODLES IN A BUN

64

In the galaxy of carb-on-carb sandwiches, one star burns brightest, outshining even the noble chip butty: the *yakisoba pan*. Yakisoba, as you may know, is stir-fried noodles, and yakisoba pan is the said noodles stuffed into a hot dog bun. My wife just gave me a look because I burst out laughing as I wrote that last sentence. Can you blame me? It is ridiculous. But it's also surprisingly good – there's a lot of texture and flavour in yakisoba, with tender noodles and crunchy veg, tangy pickles and saucy sauce. And that's exactly what makes a good sandwich: lots of contrast and something different in every bite.

MAKES 4 PORTIONS OF YAKISOBA,
WHICH IS ENOUGH FOR 6 YAKISOBA PAN

For the yakisoba
2 tablespoons oil
2 onions, sliced about 5 mm (¼ in) thick
½ hispi cabbage, cut into 1-cm (½-in) strips
6 dried shiitake mushrooms, rehydrated, destemmed
    and thinly sliced
1 tablespoon sesame oil
½ teaspoon dashi powder
3 tablespoons soy sauce
4 tablespoons tonkatsu sauce
2 tablespoons mirin
1 tablespoon sake
4 portions cooked egg noodles
40–50 g (1½–2 oz) red pickled ginger
white sesame seeds, toasted until deep golden brown
a few pinches of aonori
small handful of katsuobushi

For yakisoba pan
leftover yakisoba
hot dog buns
tonkatsu sauce
Kewpie mayo (page 46)
extra aonori and red pickled ginger (optional)

METHOD

To make the yakisoba, heat the oil in a wok or big frying pan (skillet) over a high heat, then add the onions and fry for a few minutes until they are beginning to colour. Add the cabbage and mushrooms and fry for another few minutes. Then add the sesame oil, dashi powder, soy sauce, tonkatsu sauce, mirin and sake and let the liquid reduce slightly. Then add the noodles, ginger and sesame seeds and cook for a few more minutes to let the noodles soak up the sauce. Serve in bowls topped with aonori and katsuobushi.

If you want to serve yakisoba pan, put the yakisoba into the buns. Top with a little more tonkatsu sauce, a generous squirt of Kewpie mayo and a little more aonori and pickled ginger, if you like.

東京ストリート

MIZUNA SALAD WITH SESAME-PONZU DRESSING

When I lived in Japan I had a pretty predictable weekly routine. I ate quite healthy meals throughout the week and exercised most days, but then every weekend was like one massive blowout – big izakaya meals on Friday, ramen or udon lunches on Saturday followed by another big meal on Saturday night, maybe Korean barbecue or Italian this time, all swept along in a river of glorious, glorious alcohol. When Sunday came I retreated back home to nurse hangovers ranging from fuzzy to debilitating, and for me Sunday evening was always a time for self-medicating with a feast from the conbini and pirated episodes of *Veronica Mars*. I'd go down to the 7-Eleven by my flat and stock up on sandwiches, onigiri, sweets, tea and, yes, the occasional salad – and not just as a sort of token gesture in the name of nutrition, but actually because conbini salads are so good they're even crushable with a hangover when ordinarily all I'd want is filth. My favourite was a simple leafy salad with mizuna and shredded chicken and a moreish dressing made from ground sesame and yuzu. It was refreshing, but also substantial and full of flavour.

MAKES 4 BIG SALADS (FOR A MAIN)
OR 6-8 SMALLER ONES (FOR A SIDE)

2 skinless chicken breasts
1 teaspoon sesame oil
salt and white pepper

For the sesame-ponzu dressing
25 g (1 oz/scant ¼ cup) white sesame seeds
50 g (2 oz/scant ¼ cup) tahini
2 tablespoons mirin
2 tablespoons rice vinegar
3 tablespoons yuzu juice (or lime juice)
1½ tablespoons sesame oil
1½ tablespoons vegetable oil
1 tablespoon caster (superfine) sugar
1 tablespoon soy sauce
pinch of white pepper
pinch of dashi powder or MSG (optional)
water, as needed
salt, as needed

For the salad
100 g (3½ oz) mizuna (you can use rocket instead)
½ iceberg lettuce, torn into bite-size pieces
2 tomatoes, cut into eight wedges
1 carrot, peeled and shredded
200 g (7 oz/small) tin of sweetcorn
½ cucumber, julienned

METHOD

Butterfly the chicken breasts by laying them flat on a chopping board and using a sharp knife to cut each one in half widthways, leaving the two halves un-cut and attached on one side, and opening them up like a greeting card. Rub them all over with the sesame oil, salt and pepper. Grill on medium-high for about 8 minutes, turning halfway through cooking, or until cooked through and no longer pink. Cool, then chill.

To make the dressing, toast the sesame seeds in a dry frying pan (skillet) until brown and very nutty-smelling. Remove from the heat, cool, then grind to a coarse, sandy powder with a mortar and pestle, spice mill or food processor. Combine with the tahini, mirin, vinegar, yuzu juice, sesame oil, vegetable oil, sugar, soy sauce, white pepper and dashi powder or MSG. It should be thick but pourable – if it's too thick, add a splash of water to thin it down. Taste and adjust the seasoning with salt as needed.

Shred the cooked chicken. Arrange the salad leaves in bowls and top with the tomatoes, carrot, sweetcorn, cucumber and shredded chicken. Pour over the dressing just before serving.

東京ストリート

CURRY PAN

JAPANESE CURRY-FILLED SAVOURY DOUGHNUTS

68

If something on a London restaurant menu was described as 'katsu curry doughnut,' it would be a rather novel thing. In Tokyo, just such an item has been around for nearly a century. In 1927 a baker named Toyoharu Tanaka began selling filled and fried 'Western bread', and it's likely that *kare pan* was born from this. Today, curry pan is ubiquitous – every conbini sells a decent version and they even appear in school lunches, but you can also get very nice ones made by bakers or curry restaurants.

It is best to make the curry the day before you need it so you can chill it thoroughly. You will need a probe thermometer for this one.

MAKES 6 DOUGHNUTS

For the curry
15 g (½ oz) butter
½ small onion, diced
10 g (½ oz) plain (all-purpose) flour
10 g (½ oz) curry powder
1 teaspoon garam masala
120 ml (4 fl oz/½ cup) vegetable stock
½ carrot, peeled and diced
80 g (3 oz) cauliflower, cut into small pieces
20 g (¾ oz/scant ¼ cup) peas
1 tablespoon soy sauce
1 teaspoon ketchup
hot chilli sauce, to taste (optional)

For the dough
5 g (1 teaspoon) instant yeast
60 ml (2 fl oz/¼ cup) lukewarm milk
2 large eggs, beaten
250 g (9 oz/2 cups) strong white bread flour
50 g (2 oz/heaped ⅓ cup) plain (all-purpose) flour, plus extra for dusting
3 g (½ teaspoon) salt
15 g (½ oz/1 tablespoon) caster (superfine) sugar
80 g (3 oz) butter, softened and cut into small pieces

To assemble and serve
1 egg, beaten with a splash of water or milk
40 g (1½ oz) panko
vegetable oil, for deep-frying (about 1.5 litres/ 52 fl oz/6 cups)

METHOD

To make the curry, melt the butter in a small saucepan, add the onion and fry for 5 minutes or until golden brown. Stir in the flour, curry powder and garam masala, then cook the roux for a few minutes, stirring constantly. Add the stock and bring to the boil. Add the carrot, cauliflower and peas and cook until tender, stirring frequently to ensure the sauce doesn't catch. Stir in the soy sauce, ketchup and chilli sauce, if using, then remove from the heat and chill thoroughly.

To make the dough, stir together the yeast and milk until the yeast dissolves, then stir the mixture into the eggs. Place the flours, salt and sugar in a mixing bowl (use an electric mixer with a dough hook, if you have one) and mix lightly, then add the liquid ingredients. Mix by hand or on a low speed for 2 minutes, then turn the speed up to medium and mix for another 7 minutes, or knead on a floured surface for 15 minutes. Add the butter and knead or mix for a further 5 minutes until no chunks of butter remain and the dough is very smooth and soft. Wrap the dough in cling film (plastic wrap) and chill for at least 2 hours.

Divide the dough into 8 equal pieces and roll them into balls. Roll the balls out into rounds about 10 cm (4 in) across, then flatten out the edges a little (each round should be a little bit thicker at the centre). Place a big spoonful of curry in the centre of each round, then fold over and press the edges together firmly to tightly seal in the curry (if they open even a little in the oil, the curry will come gushing out). Crimp the sealed edges of each doughnut using a fold-and-roll motion like making a pasty, then turn the doughnuts onto a lightly oiled tray, sealed side down. Transfer to the fridge and chill for at least 1 hour.

Place the panko on a tray or plate. Brush each doughnut with the egg wash, then roll through the panko. Cover the doughnuts loosely in cling film (plastic wrap) and leave to prove in a warm place for 1–2 hours, or until they have nearly doubled in size.

Heat the oil to 160°C (320°F) and carefully lower the doughnuts into the oil, 2 or 3 at a time, sealed-side down. After a few seconds, flip the doughnuts over so the seam is now at the top (this will help prevent them from over-inflating, which causes the bread to be too hollow). Fry for 8 minutes, turning frequently, until they are golden brown. Leave to cool slightly before serving.

LOCAL

GODZILLA ゴジラ

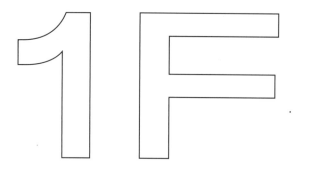

TOKYO LOCAL

SPECIALTIES OF THE CITY

Japanese floor-numbering conventions follow the American model, so the first floor is what would be called the ground floor in the UK. And it's here, or street level, that you'll find many of the iconic foods most closely associated with Tokyo.

Like a lot of capital cities, Tokyo doesn't have many local specialties to call its own. Tokyo's hyper-developed land means there isn't much in the way of agriculture, and its status as *the* cultural and economic centre of Japan means that it has never had the need to create its own food identities to stand out the way smaller cities have. Tokyo's true 'local food' is probably global food due to its sheer diversity.

However, once you start to explore Tokyo's history and some of its less-travelled districts, you do start to discover unique specialities that are either closely associated with Tokyo, or rarely found outside Tokyo, or both. These include ramen, both old-school and new-school, earthy soul food dishes based on creatures found in Tokyo's brackish rivers and bays, and iconic Japanese dishes with origins in the centuries-old street food culture of Tokyo – or perhaps more accurately, of Edo.

Edo is the old name for Tokyo, which translates very un-romantically as 'estuary', or maybe more fancifully as 'bay doorway'. (Tokyo literally means 'eastern capital', an equally functional and kind of blasé name for one of the most vibrant cities in the world, but hey ho.) Edo was the seat of the Tokugawa shogunate, the ruling military dynasty of Japan from the beginning of the 17th century to the middle of the 19th, and although it wasn't officially the capital of the country, in reality the political, cultural and economic power that was held by Kyoto for centuries before dramatically shifted to Edo during this time. A lot of this has to do with the shogun's practice of what was called *sankin kotai*, or alternate attendance, which required the lords of Japan's many domains to reside in Edo for a certain period of time each year, which helped to consolidate power in Edo while destabilising the rest of the country. It was all very clever, and as a result of this autocratic centralisation, the country experienced an enforced 'pax Edo' for almost three centuries.

This period of relative peace left a lot of previously very busy soldiers with little to do, and the samurai became a sort of reluctant leisure class. Higher-ranking officials with larger stipends could engage in more highbrow pursuits of the *ukiyo*, the 'floating world' of urban idleness, such as tea ceremony, *kabuki* theatre, and prostitution elevated to an art form. Lower ranks had to engage in more frugal entertainments such as binge drinking, racketeering and pornographic woodblock prints. But they could also enjoy the emerging phenomenon of cheap street food - which included, by the early 19th century, Japan's most emblematic dish: *edomae sushi*.

EDOMAE SUSHI

TRADITIONAL TOKYO-STYLE SUSHI

74

Let's break this down. Sushi is, of course, sushi, but it's original, obsolete meaning is 'sour-tasting'. This refers to the flavour of vinegared rice, which is now used primarily for its tangy, mouthwatering flavour, but was originally done to preserve both the rice and fish. The funny thing is that although sushi is so closely associated with freshness, proto-sushi was anything but. In fact, sushi comes from the same culinary lineage as Southeast Asian fish sauce and other salted, preserved fish products; the original Japanese sushi (now called *narezushi*) was fish preserved by the salinity and acidity produced by fermenting it with salt and rice. You can still find this primordial sushi in a few places in Japan, and while I haven't tried it, by all accounts it is pretty punchy stuff.

The use of vinegar to either supplement or entirely replace the lactic acid that once preserved the fish was already practised by the beginning of the Edo period – this made the process simpler and quicker, while increasing its efficacy and shelf life. But it wasn't until the second half of the 18th century that chefs began to abandon the preservation part of the sushi process entirely and simply serve fresh fish on top of vinegary rice. This innovation is widely attributed to the east Edo-based chef Hanaya Yohei, although in reality there were probably a number of shops producing similar dishes, not only in Edo but also in Osaka. 'Edomae', by the way, refers to Edo Bay – the original source of the fresh fish that adorned sushi and which is still used as an indicator of traditional methods and quality ingredients, even when they don't actually come from anywhere near Tokyo Bay.

By the 1830s, this new form of sushi had caught on and street stalls around the capital sprung up, serving inexpensive sushi to Edo's working (or out-of-work) classes. Early sushi was pretty rough-and-ready stuff and the new government installed after the Meiji Revolution in 1868 quickly cracked down on dicey sushi stalls, citing public health concerns. But sushi was already well established in Tokyo by this point and the dispersal of Tokyoites to other parts of the country following the Great Kanto Earthquake in 1923 helped spread the dish across Japan, creating a national dish out of what was once local.

But edomae sushi is still considered a thing to eat specifically in Tokyo, especially in the surrounds of Tsukiji, the hectic, smelly fish market so big and so bustling it's like a whole other city in and of itself. Locals and tourists alike know that this is an excellent area to nab some great-value sushi, as the shops here are numerous and no-frills, while the fish couldn't be fresher. It's typical for these shops to have queues around breakfast time, full of sushi fans eager to get their hands on just-landed seafood. In October 2018, Tsukiji Market closed and Tokyo's wholesale seafood operation moved to shiny new premises in Toyosu. Only time will tell if the surrounding area will become a hotspot for bargain breakfast sushi but, even if it doesn't, there will still be plenty of places to find great sushi across the capital.

It's a little odd to give a recipe for edomae sushi – which is most commonly *nigiri* sushi – because it's really more about ingredients and technique than a recipe (except for the rice itself, which is very important, of course). So what follows is more of a guide to how to make the best sushi you can at home, with a few tips to get the most out of your rice, fish and seasonings – you may be surprised at how amazing you can make your sushi with a little practise and some top-quality fish.

Where to find
Sushidokoro Yamazaki 寿司所やまざき Tsukiji Shijo, 〒104-0045, sushi-yamazaki.com

SUSHI RICE

SHARI

Sushi *neta* (toppings) usually get all the glory, but the *shari* (rice) is just as important, if not more so, in making great sushi. Think of a sandwich – you can have all sorts of great fillings, but they'll all be worthless if you don't use good bread as well. Great sushi rice should be:

76

Perfectly cooked
not too soft and not too firm

Perfectly sticky
not gummy, starchy or dry

Perfectly seasoned
with enough acid, sugar
and salt to enliven the palate
and create a mouthwatering,
moreish quality

Perfectly warm
never cold, and not hot, but
just above body temperature

Perfectly shaped
not mashed together but also not
so loose it falls apart en route
from your plate to your mouth

You've heard how it takes years and years to become a sushi chef? Yeah, well this is why – cooking great sushi rice takes a LOT of practise. I will provide a recipe for how to make the rice, but a lot of it will come down to your senses and intuition, and a bit of trial and error. When you cook the rice, be sure to taste it and feel it every step of the way: Is the rice the right texture? Will it be too soft when I add the vinegar? Is it too soft to begin with? Will it be too hard if it cools down a bit? If so, adjust the cooking process accordingly with less or more water, time or heat. Is it too sticky? Wash it a bit more next time? Is the texture uneven? Be sure to soak the rice ahead of time. When you're ready to make the sushi, check it again: Is it the right temperature? Is it holding together nicely, with distinct individual grains and without a gluey coating? When you're shaping it, feel it and press it together just until you're confident it will hold together. Chances are you can't quit your day job to train as a sushi chef, but just taking a little time to make your sushi rice with care and attention will get you pretty far.

THIS WILL MAKE ENOUGH RICE
FOR ABOUT 20 PIECES OF NIGIRI

300 g (10½ oz/1½ cups) rice
390 ml (13¾ fl oz/1½ cups) water
2 tablespoons rice vinegar – for really good quality rice, use a good-quality rice vinegar with a proper fermented rice flavour (brown rice vinegars are excellent)
2 tablespoons caster (superfine) sugar
1 tablespoon salt

METHOD

Wash your rice very, very thoroughly – get the water as clear as you have the patience for. I find it easiest to do this under a running tap, instead of in a pan. Put the rice in a pan and cover with enough water to come 1 cm (½ in) above the surface of the rice and leave to soak for an hour. Meanwhile, stir together the vinegar, sugar and salt until the sugar and salt completely dissolve. Drain the rice, then add the measured water. Place over a high heat and bring to a low boil, then reduce the heat to low, place a lid on the pan and cook for 15 minutes. Remove from the heat and tip the rice out into a wide, shallow bowl. Drizzle over the sushi vinegar and use a slicing and turning motion with a rice paddle or a spatula to gently but thoroughly coat all the rice with the vinegar (make sure you don't smash the rice). Cover loosely with a tea towel and leave to cool and absorb the seasoning. When the rice is just barely warm to the touch, it is ready to use.

東
京
ロ
ー
カ
ル

SUSHI TOPPINGS AND SEASONINGS

NETA

78

If you want to make great sushi, you really need to get the best quality fish you can find, and this is very likely to be from the fish counter or freezer section of your local Japanese supermarket. The fish here is typically caught and processed in Japan, specifically for sushi and sashimi, then flash-frozen and shipped abroad. The result is fish that's expensive, but also reliably excellent quality – and not only that, it's easy to use because it's already been cut and trimmed into neat fillets or blocks, so all you have to do is slice off sushi-sized pieces and you're ready to go.

Alternatively, if you know a really excellent local fishmonger, you can potentially get even better quality fish that will probably come in cheaper as well. Tell them you need fish for sushi and they should be able to tell you what's in season and of good quality at the market, they should get it to you fresh as a daisy, and they should be able to clean and trim it however you need it. What's fun about this is that you may be able to get some interesting local alternatives to the stuff that's been shipped over from Japan, which can often have fantastic flavour and texture because it will be so fresh. My favourite sushi restaurants in the UK do this – why bother with fish that's been flown from halfway around the world when we're surrounded by excellent seafood off our own coasts?

The two main seasonings for sushi are soy sauce and wasabi. Both of these need to be of good quality if you are trying to achieve sushi greatness. There are many, many, many types of soy sauce to choose from, but a good, naturally brewed and preferably long-aged shoyu will do nicely for all kinds of sushi – just don't overdo it. I also personally like lighter soy sauces like usukuchi or even the unusual shiro shoyu, a so called 'white' soy sauce made with a higher amount of wheat so it has a much lighter colour and flavour. Sushi masters in Japan will usually blend various soy sauces to achieve a

desired flavour and consistency, and some will mix them with other seasonings such as sake, mirin, kombu and katsuobushi, to further fine-tune its flavour and add depth and complexity – many even have different blends for different neta. I would very much recommend adding a tiny bit of sugar or mirin to your soy sauce, just to round it out a bit and take the edge off the salinity. And a little katsuobushi infused into the sauce does wonders to amplify the neta's natural umami. Whatever you choose to season your fish, I'd recommend brushing it onto the top of the fish rather than using it as a dip – you get a lighter, more even seasoning this way, and you don't risk soaking the rice.

As for wasabi, the main thing to look out for is whether or not your wasabi is real or not – most of it is horseradish dyed green, so check the label. Real wasabi is labelled '*hon* wasabi' in Japanese, and it's less intense and a bit sweeter than the fake stuff. I think the frozen wasabi has a better flavour than the stuff in a tube, as well. But the real primo wasabi is, of course, the fresh root itself – it's rare and expensive, but the flavour is incomparable. There's a fruity aroma and almost potato-like fluffy texture to it you just don't really get from the processed stuff, and its heat is beautifully restrained. If you're serious about sushi, it is worth seeking out and splurging on, at least once. Even fresh wasabi should be applied with a delicate hand; all but the most robust of neta will be wiped out by too much of it. That said, oily, strongly-flavoured fish like mackerel or sardines work beautifully with a more generous smear of wasabi, and in fact this kind of fish will require bolder seasonings generally, such as grated ginger, finely sliced spring onions (scallions) or chives, shredded *myoga* (Japanese ginger blossom), tart citrus or even a bit of chilli.

SHAPING AND DEVOURING SUSHI

So you've got your rice, you've got your toppings, and you've got your seasonings. Now all you have to do is put them together, then put them in your face. In many ways this is the easy part, but it still requires some practise.

First of all, slice the fish – always against the grain, but how thick and wide is up to you. Firmer fish like sea bass and sea bream should generally be sliced more thinly, so they aren't chewy, while tender fish like salmon, tuna and mackerel can be thicker. Some fish, like little sardines, don't need to be sliced at all, but you may have to score their skin so that it breaks more easily between the teeth. Only slice as much as you will need – with each slice you create more surface area, which makes the fish more prone to lose flavour, discolour, and eventually spoil.

Have a bowl of room-temperature, lightly salted water handy. To shape the sushi, wet your hands with the salted water, grab a little handful of rice, and compress it in your palm, with a motion like clenching your fist but more gentle. When the rice is loosely packed and about 2 cm (¾ in) wide and 4 cm (1½ in) long, use your fingertip to apply a small amount of wasabi to the top of the rice, then place a slice of fish on top of that. Cup the sushi in the palm of your non-dominant hand, and use your index and middle fingers on your dominant hand to press down along the entire length of the sushi while clenching the palm of your other hand to firmly squash everything together ('nigiri', by the way, means 'pressed'). Brush with the soy sauce or soy sauce blend of your choice, add any additional toppings you might want, and devour immediately, while the rice is still warm. Lean back as you chew, close your eyes and focus on the perfect harmony and contrast of cold, fresh, supple seafood with warm, tangy, toothsome rice. Smile deeply, have a sip of beer or sake or tea, eat some pickled ginger and repeat until satisfied.

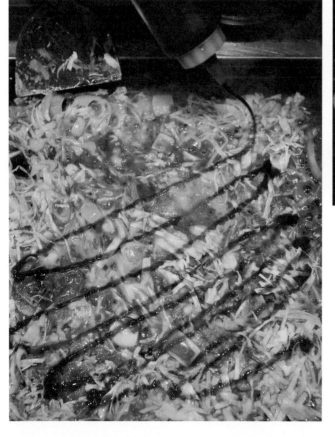

MONJAYAKI

GRIDDLED GOO

You never forget your first *monjayaki* – because it's so weird.

Monjayaki is a speciality of Tsukishima, a working class neighbourhood of Tokyo's east side 'old downtown' built on an artificial island constructed as a sort of by-product from the dredging of a shipping channel through Tokyo Bay. Tsukishima is now home to over 70 monjayaki restaurants, but you can find it all around eastern Tokyo. I first tried it in Asakusa in 2005; I didn't really understand what I was ordering, and I assumed it was just a local variety of okonomiyaki, the famous savoury pancake. And it sort of is ... but it's like okonomiyaki that's gone wrong. While okonomiyaki batter is thick and solidifies when it's griddled, monjayaki batter is incredibly thin and, instead, it just becomes a kind of thick goo as it's cooked. Like okonomiyaki, it's cooked at the table and eaten directly off the griddle. The waitress at the restaurant where I was eating could tell I was super-confused by this bubbling mass before me, and she had to come over and explain how to eat it – basically, when it's the consistency of melted cheese or a very thick sauce, you just scrape off mouthfuls of it with tiny spatulas and tuck in. It is honestly one of the weirdest things I've ever eaten – but it's also really delicious. The consistency is awfully hard to describe, but it isn't unpleasant, and it's actually quite fun to cook – and, also like okonomiyaki, you can put whatever you want in it. This recipe is for my favourite combo: kimchi, sweetcorn and cheese. The cheese in particular is fantastic, because it doubles down on the gooeyness of the dish while also creating little crispy bits at the edges as the liquid cooks off. You will need a griddle for this dish – an electric one is handy, so you can cook and eat this at the table, Tsukishima-style.

SERVES 2

500 ml (17 fl oz/2 cups) water
4 tablespoons plain (all-purpose) flour
1 tablespoon soy sauce
½ teaspoon dashi powder
½ hispi cabbage or flat cabbage, shredded
100 g (3½ oz) kimchi, roughly chopped
150–200 g (5–7 oz/small) tin of sweetcorn, drained
4 spring onions (scallions), thinly sliced
1 tablespoon vegetable oil
100 g (3½ oz) mozzarella, grated
beni shoga, as needed (optional)
4 tablespoons *okonomi* sauce or
    Worcestershire sauce
1 tablespoon aonori

METHOD

In a mixing bowl, stir together the water, flour, soy sauce, dashi powder, cabbage, kimchi and sweetcorn. Save a handful of the spring onions to use as a topping later, then add the rest to the mixture. Heat your griddle over a high heat and add the oil, then tip in the batter – it will spread out and cover the entire griddle. As it cooks it will thicken, and when it is the consistency of a thick gravy, sprinkle on the cheese, beni shoga (if using) and reserved spring onions. When the whole mixture thickens to a sticky, melted cheese-like texture, add the sauce and the aonori. Now you simply scrape mouthfuls of it off the griddle and enjoy. I know it's weird. But this is how they do it in Tsukishima!

Where to find
Tsukishima Monja Street 月島もんじゃストリート
Tsukishima, 〒104-0052, monja.gr.jp

東
京
ロ
ー
カ
ル

SOBA

BUCKWHEAT NOODLES

82

Today, Tokyo's dominant noodle is ramen, but this wasn't always the case – back in the Edo period, soba reigned supreme. Buckwheat is easier to grow in Japan than rice, which makes it cheap, and therefore soba noodles became a street-food staple among the working classes in old Edo, where vendors would sell it for mere pennies a bowl. Like most foods in Japanese cuisine, it has by now been fussed over and fancied up in all kinds of ways, but I think I like it best as just simple, unpretentious comfort food (you can still get a bowl for ¥400 in some places, which is amazing). Good-quality dried soba noodles are easy to come by these days, but it's also not that hard to make them from scratch, which allows you to cut them to any thickness you like (I like a nice, chunky soba noodle) and also control the buckwheat-to-wheat flour ratio to your liking.

You'll need a long rolling pin for this and a knife with a flat edge (or you could probably use a pasta machine).

MAKES 4-6 PORTIONS OF NOODLES

400 g (14 oz/3 cups) buckwheat flour
100 g (3½ oz/heaped ¾ cup) plain (all-purpose) flour, plus extra for dusting
250 ml (8½ fl oz/1 cup) water

METHOD

Combine the flours in a wide, deep bowl, then add half of the water. Bring the dough together with your fingers until it starts to clump up and form a sandy texture. Add most of the remaining water (you may not need it all) and continue to mix until it forms a coarse, dry dough. The dough should be quite stiff, so only add as much water as you need to get it to all stick together. Knead the dough for at least 10 minutes until it becomes smooth and supple. Shape it into a ball, cover with cling film (plastic wrap) and leave to rest and hydrate for 20–30 minutes.

Generously flour your work surface, then squash the dough ball down into a disc and spread it out with your hands to a thickness of about 1 cm (½ in). Use a rolling pin to roll it out further, rotating the dough 90 degrees periodically so it forms 4 corners as you roll – the dough should become a big square. Continue rolling until it is 2–3 mm (⅛ in) thick, then dust the surface of the dough with more flour and fold it over onto itself, then again and then one more time, so you have 8 layers of dough stacked up in total. Use a knife to cut the dough into noodles – they can be as thin as 2 mm (⅛ in) but as wide as 1 cm (½ in). Cook immediately in boiling water until the noodles float (just a minute or two), or spread them out and let them dry (but you just can't beat fresh soba). Rinse them with cold water and serve chilled with strong tsuyu, spring onions and shredded nori, or serve hot in a light dashi with soy sauce, grated daikon, spring onions (scallions) and a soft-boiled egg.

東京ローカル

Where to find
Tamawarai 玉笑
Meiji Jingumae, Shibuya-ku 〒150-0001

HANETSUKI GYOZA

PORK POTSTICKER DUMPLINGS WITH CRISPY 'WINGS'

If there is a heaven, it is filled with *gyoza*. Maybe that's why I like Tokyo so much – there seems to be gyoza everywhere you turn. A staple of izakaya, ramen shops, home kitchens, festivals, Chinese restaurants, supermarkets, street stalls (basically wherever food is sold), gyoza is one of the most popular items in Japanese gastronomy. In recent years, it has begun to attract the same level of obsession as ramen, with chefs finding clever new ways to take their gyoza to the next level and demand the attention of fickle gyoza geeks. One simple but nonetheless impressive way to embellish gyoza is to make it *hanetsuki* style. Hanetsuki literally means 'with wings', and it refers to a light, lacy, crispy rice paper-like crust that forms along the outside of the gyoza when starchy water is added to the pan and left to evaporate away. I actually made hanetsuki gyoza for the first time by accident when I added a bit of floury water I was using to seal the dumplings to the pan to steam them, and then spent months trying to recreate the same effect. This is the recipe I came up with, and it may take you some practise, but even if the wings don't come out the first time (or even the third or tenth time), it doesn't matter – you'll still end up with tasty gyoza, which is never, ever a bad thing.

MAKES ABOUT 24 GYOZA

250 g (9 oz) well-fatted minced (ground) pork
4 garlic cloves, finely grated
2-cm (¾-in) piece of ginger root, peeled and finely grated
15 g (½ oz) nira, finely sliced
80 g (3 oz) Chinese leaf (Napa cabbage), finely chopped
3 g (½ teaspoon) salt
¼ teaspoon white pepper
24 gyoza wrappers (note: gyoza wrappers usually come in packs of 24 or 30; this recipe will make 30 gyoza if you just use a tiny bit less filling in each one)
10 g (½ oz) cornflour (cornstarch), plus a little more for dusting
10 g (½ oz) plain (all-purpose) flour
150 ml (5 fl oz/scant ⅔ cup) cold water

For the dipping sauce
4 tablespoons soy sauce
2 tablespoons rice vinegar
1 teaspoon chilli oil or sesame oil

METHOD

First of all, this will require a very reliable non-stick pan or well-seasoned frying pan (skillet) with a lid. Don't even attempt these without one or the gyoza won't cook properly and the wings won't release from the pan.

Combine the pork, garlic, ginger, nira, Chinese leaf, sea salt and white pepper, and mix well. To assemble the gyoza, have your gyoza wrappers and a bowl of cold water at hand, with the wrappers unwrapped but covered loosely with a damp cloth or piece of paper towel (if the wrappers dry out, they're extremely difficult to seal). Lay out a few wrappers at a time and moisten their edges with your fingertips dipped in the water. Add a small spoonful of the filling to the centre of each wrapper, then fold them over the filling and crimp one side while firmly pressing it onto the other side to seal. This will take some practise, but don't worry if your crimping skills aren't 'gyoza master' level. Some cooks don't crimp at all, and un-crimped or awkwardly crimped gyoza still taste delicious. Keep the gyoza lined up on a tray dusted with a little cornflour and covered with a damp piece of paper towel as you go along.

Stir together the soy sauce, vinegar and chilli or sesame oil to make the dipping sauce.

To cook, prepare your starch slurry by stirring together the flours and water. It should resemble milk. Pour a little frying oil in your non-stick pan and wipe it around the surface with paper towel so that only a thin film of oil remains (too much oil will cause the slurry to bubble, which makes it difficult to hold together). Heat the pan over a medium-high heat until it feels quite warm when you hold your hand over it, then add the gyoza, seal-side up, in a sunflower/pinwheel pattern – you will probably be able to fit all the gyoza in the pan at once, but not to worry if not. Just make sure all the gyoza are snuggled up to each other, with no gaps between them, otherwise you'll risk breaking the wings when you remove them from the pan.

Cook the gyoza for 1 minute. Give the cornflour liquid a good stir to mix in anything that might have settled to the bottom, then pour about 3–4 tablespoons of the liquid into the pan. The slurry should cover the bottom of the pan completely and surround all the gyoza. Immediately place a lid on the pan, turn the heat up to high and leave to steam for 3 minutes. Remove the lid and continue to cook to let all the liquid evaporate. When the pan is totally dry, a light, thin crust should

東
京
ロ
ー
カ
ル

84

5F
4F
3F
2F
1F
B1F
B2F

have formed – you will be able to tell when it's done because no part of it will still be bubbling and the crust will have curled away slightly from the edges of the pan.

To serve, it is best to have a plate that fits inside your frying pan (skillet) so it can be rested on top of the gyoza in the pan. Lay the plate upside-down on top of the gyoza, then carefully invert the pan and plate. Say a little prayer to the gyoza gods and carefully lift the pan away. With a little luck, you will have a gorgeous platter of hanetsuki gyoza. Enjoy piping hot with a celebratory sake, then steel yourself to make more on a regular basis – these will be popular!

```
Where to find

Dailian  大連
Azabu Juban, 〒106-0045, asian-table.jp
```

85

HARUKIYA-STYLE OLD-SCHOOL TOKYO SHOYU RAMEN

Like so many of the world's most beloved dishes, the story of ramen is a story of hardship. Originally a staple of marginalised Chinese immigrant communities in Japan, ramen caught on with the wider Japanese population – and then, the whole world – in part because of its incredibly high satisfaction-to-price ratio.

I recently re-watched the 1985 classic 'ramen Western' film *Tampopo*. It's a beautiful film about food and how it affects us and connects us, centring on a single mother as she struggles to perfect her ramen, and the savvy John Wayne-esque trucker who becomes her mentor. The amount of effort she puts into her ramen is deeply affecting, especially if you happen to run a ramen shop yourself: an endeavour fraught with trials of endurance and emotional devastation. There's a lot to relate to in *Tampopo*'s story, but what struck me the most the last time I watched it was the price of ramen they mentioned: ¥400. That was in 1985 and you can *still* get a very decent bowl of ramen for ¥600! For me there is something beautiful about that, and not just because I'm a cheap bastard. To make something so delicious, so nourishing, so filling, and keep it so affordable, can only come from a labour of love. I mean how else can you expect to get so much flavour from bones, water, flour and a few simple seasonings and toppings? Ramen is a kind of magic.

This recipe is based on the ramen found at Haruki-ya, a legendary ramen shop that has been operating in the western Tokyo neighbourhood of Ogikubo since 1954. Their ramen is, in my opinion, still the best example of a classic Tokyo-style shoyu ramen to be found – a clear yet substantial broth based on chicken and pork bones, glistening with droplets of chicken fat, seasoned with soy sauce and dried sardines, and filled out with wavy noodles, lean pork and a few traditional toppings. Like all good ramen, this recipe takes time, but the end result is so much more than the sum of its parts. Make it for someone you love – even if that someone is yourself.

SERVES 4

For the broth
1.8 litres (60 fl oz/7½ cups) water
100 g (3½ oz) chicken feet
1 chicken back
6 chicken wings (whole wings, not segments)
1 pig's trotter, chopped up (ask your butcher)
20 g (¾ oz) iriko (dried sardines), guts and heads removed
1 onion, quartered
50 g (2 oz) piece of ginger root, sliced (no need to peel)
10 g (½ oz) kombu (about a 10-cm (4-in) square), rinsed
10 g (½ oz) katsuobushi

For the chashu
4 tablespoons soy sauce
2 tablespoons light soft brown sugar
500 g (1 lb 2 oz) pork loin

To serve
2 tablespoons dark soy sauce (koikuchi or tamari)
3 tablespoons light soy sauce (usukuchi)
2 tablespoons mirin
1 tablespoon sea salt flakes, or more to taste
4 portions medium-thick, wavy ramen noodles (fresh is best)
80 g (3 oz) menma
2 spring onions (scallions), thinly sliced
1 sheet of nori, cut into 4 squares

東京ローカル

88

METHOD

To make the broth, preheat the oven to 120°C (250°F/gas ¼). Combine the water, chicken feet, chicken back, wings, trotter, iriko, onion and ginger in a large stock pot or casserole. Gradually bring to a low boil over a medium heat, skimming the scum off the surface as it begins to bubble. Simmer for about half an hour, or until no new scum rises to the top, skimming constantly. Top up the water to cover the bones, if needed, cover with a lid or kitchen foil, then transfer to the oven. Leave to simmer in the oven for 5 hours.

Remove the bones (you can eat the meat from the wings, if you like) and pass the broth through a fine sieve. Add the kombu and the katsuobushi and leave to infuse for 1 hour. Pass through a sieve again and measure – you will need 1.4 litres (50 fl oz/6 cups) of broth in total, so simply top up with water as needed. Chill completely, then remove the solidified fat from the surface of the broth and reserve. Use a ladle to scoop out the broth and transfer to a separate container, leaving behind any debris on the bottom. (The broth should be very clear.)

To make the chashu, preheat the oven to 140°C (275°F/gas ½). Stir together the soy sauce and sugar until the sugar dissolves. Score the surface of the pork and rub the sweet soy mixture all over, then transfer to the oven and roast just until the internal temperature reaches 57°C (134°F) – this should take no more than 30 minutes. (If you don't have a probe thermometer, prod the pork – it should still feel fairly supple. And remember, if the pork is undercooked, you can always cook it more, but if if's overcooked, there's no going back. So err on the side of rare and take it out as soon as you think it might be done!) Chill the pork completely.

To serve, bring the broth to a simmer and add the soy sauces, mirin and salt. Taste and adjust the seasoning as you like. Prepare a large saucepan full of boiling water. Thinly slice the chashu. Melt the reserved fat from the broth in a small saucepan or in the microwave. Cook the noodles in the boiling water according to the package instructions, ensuring that they have a good bite to them. Drain well. Divide the broth evenly among the 4 bowls, then place the noodles in the broth. Top each bowl with a slice of chashu, the menma, some spring onions and a spoonful or two of the melted fat. Place the nori squares on the side of each bowl, slightly submerged in the broth. Enjoy piping hot and don't forget to slurp!

東京ローカル

Where to find
Harukiya 春木屋
Ogikubo, 〒167-0043, haruki-ya.co.jp

TAISHOKEN-STYLE TSUKEMEN

DIPPING RAMEN

90

Udon and soba have been served cold with a dipping sauce on the side for centuries, but ramen wasn't given the same treatment until the 1970s. 'Tsukemen,' as it has come to be known, is widely attributed to chef Kazuo Yamagishi of the ramen shop Taishoken, who decided to sell dipping ramen as a special after inquisitive customers observed him enjoying his customary working snack: leftover noodles dipped in a mug of hot broth with plenty of soy sauce. What ultimately went on the menu was a sort of deconstructed yet heightened ramen: the noodles were super-thick and toothsome, chilled down and served on the side to preserve their texture, while the broth was rich, dense and highly seasoned, featuring an unusual combination of flavourful ingredients including sugar, vinegar and various types of dried fish. The mixture of meat and seafood that Yamagishi developed would come to be known as 'double soup', a trend that came to dominate the Tokyo ramen scene in the early 2000s. Tsukemen itself also caught on in a big way, with thousands of imitators springing up over the years, to the extent that it is now considered its own distinct genre of ramen rather than just an idiosyncratic novelty.

To me, tsukemen is brilliant because it solves a lot of ramen problems. You don't have to worry about the noodles going soft, because they aren't soaked in the broth. You don't have to worry about scalding your mouth, because the temperature is naturally regulated when you dip the cold noodles into the hot soup. And you don't have to worry about toppings losing their texture or freshness, or otherwise getting swamped by the broth, because they can be served on the side as well. It's really a brilliant invention. I actually met Yamagishi-san back in 2008 – he was sitting outside his original Ikebukuro shop, shaking hands with customers and posing for photos – but I didn't really understand how much of a legend he was at the time. He's dead now, but if you can hear me up there in ramen heaven, THANK YOU, Yamagishi-san, for giving us all the gift of tsukemen.

SERVES 4

For the broth

2.5 litres (85 fl oz/10½ cups) water, plus more, as needed
1 kg (2 lb 4 oz) pork thigh bones – ask your butcher to cut them in half lengthways to expose the marrow
1 chicken back
1 pig's trotter, chopped (ask your butcher)
50 g (2 oz) chicken feet
50 g (2 oz) chicken skin (ask your butcher)
1 leek, halved
1 large onion, halved
1 carrot, washed and halved
1 bulb garlic, halved
40 g (1½ oz) iriko, guts and heads removed
50 g (2 oz) piece of ginger root, thinly sliced (no need to peel)
100 g (3½ oz) pork back fat, finely chopped
10 g (½ oz) kombu (about a 10-cm (4-in) square), rinsed
20 g (¾ oz) katsuobushi
120 ml (4 fl oz/½ cup) dark soy sauce (koikuchi)
2 tablespoons caster (superfine) sugar
2 tablespoons rice vinegar
½ teaspoon finely ground pepper
¼ teaspoon Japanese or Korean chilli powder

To serve

4 portions ramen noodles – get the thickest ones you can find
soy sauce, as needed
4 slices of Chashu (page 87)
2 eggs, hard-boiled, peeled and halved
80 g (3 oz) menma
2 spring onions (scallions), thinly sliced
4 slices of naruto
½ sheet of nori, cut into 4 rectangles

METHOD

To make the broth, combine the water, pork bones, chicken back, trotter, chicken feet and chicken skin in a large stock pot. Gradually bring to the boil over a medium heat, skimming the scum off the surface as it begins to bubble. Simmer for about half an hour, or until no new scum rises to the top, skimming constantly. Top up the water to cover the bones and continue to boil on a high heat for 3 hours, topping up the water as necessary to keep everything covered.

Add the leek, onion, carrot, garlic, iriko and ginger, reduce the heat to medium and continue to boil for another hour, without topping up the water. Remove from the heat and stir in the prepared back fat, then the kombu and katsuobushi. Leave to infuse for 1 hour, then pass the broth through a sieve and measure it – you should have 1 litre (34 fl oz/4 cups) of broth, so boil to reduce the liquid as needed. Add the soy sauce, sugar, vinegar, pepper and chilli powder and stir until the sugar dissolves.

To serve, boil the noodles until tender, then drain and rinse very well under cold running water – you need to get all the starch off to keep them from sticking together. Divide the noodles among 4 small bowls. Bring the broth to the boil and taste it – it should be saltier than normal ramen broth to season the noodles properly, so add a bit more soy sauce if you think it needs it. Ensuring the broth is as hot as possible, ladle it into separate bowls just before serving. Taishoken and most other tsukemen shops serve the toppings in the broth – but I prefer them on the noodles. It's up to you, really. To eat, grab a mouthful of noodles with your chopsticks, dip and swirl them through the broth and slurp. When all the noodles are gone, add a little bit of boiling water to the remaining broth to dilute the seasoning, and drink it down.

Where to find
Taishoken 大勝軒
Higashi Ikebukuro, 〒167-0043, tai-sho-ken.com

JIRO-STYLE RAMEN

EXTREMELY LARGE AND RICH RAMEN WITH PORK AND VEGETABLES

You may have heard of the Jiro who dreams of sushi, a chef whose obsessive devotion to his craft has made him the subject of a documentary film? Well there's another Jiro in town, and he dreams of ramen.

Ramen Jiro is one of the culinary wonders of Tokyo, an absolute must for ramenheads or anybody else interested in experiencing gastronomic (and gastrointestinal) extremes. Ramen Jiro is unique in many ways – some people say it isn't even ramen, but a distinct dish called Jiro – but perhaps its defining characteristic is simply obscene excessiveness. It is over the top in every way, a hysterically exaggerated caricature of ramen's more indulgent aspects: intimidatingly voluminous, grotesquely fatty, sharply seasoned with MSG and soy sauce, chock-full of thick, coarse, slippery noodles and piled high with a veritable Matterhorn of bean sprouts, cabbage, minced garlic and boiled pork. This is ramen that does not mess around, and it is not for everybody. But if you can stomach it (I barely can, to be honest, and I love fatty food) you'll be rewarded with an almost psychedelic ramen experience, dizzyingly delicious and profoundly satisfying. You'll also be rewarded with a tummy ache.

The bottom line is that Jiro is a very special bowl of ramen, deserving of its loyal cult following and many imitators. If you're the kind of person who can never find a bowl of ramen quite rich enough, big enough or salty enough to satisfy you – try Jiro. At the very least, it's impossible to be underwhelmed by it.

This recipe includes hand-made ramen noodles, which require kansui. Kansui is lye water, similar to what is used to make pretzels to give them their characteristic mahogany colour. In ramen, it alters the flour to give the finished noodles their characteristic 'bounce,' and it is essential to authentic ramen. You can find it at Asian supermarkets or online.

You will need very large bowls to serve Jiro – at least 900 ml (30 fl oz/3¾ cups) capacity.

SERVES 2

For the broth and chashu
2 litres (70 fl oz/8 cups) water
500 g (1 lb 2 oz) pork spine bones, cut in half
500 g (1 lb 2 oz) pork thigh bones, cut in half
250 g (9 oz) pork back fat, or skin with plenty of fat on it
100 g (3½ oz) minced (ground) pork
4 tablespoons soy sauce, plus more to taste
1½ tablespoons MSG
1½ tablespoons mirin, plus more to taste
1 leek, halved
1 carrot, peeled and halved
1 bulb garlic, halved
50 g (2 oz) piece of ginger root, peeled and sliced
500 g (1 lb 2 oz) skinless pork collar, neck or shoulder, rolled and tied

For the noodles
1 teaspoon kansui
¼ teaspoon salt
120 ml (4 fl oz/½ cup) water
240 g (8½ oz/scant 2 cups) plain (all-purpose) flour, plus extra for dusting

To serve
100 g (3½ oz) back fat, cut into big chunks (optional)
300 g (10½ oz) bean sprouts
½ hispi or flat cabbage, coarsely chopped or torn
chashu, sliced about 2 cm (¾ in) thick and kept warm
8–10 garlic cloves (or more, to taste), finely chopped

95

東
京
ロ
ー
カ
ル

5F

4F

3F

2F

1F

B1F

B2F

96

METHOD

To make the broth, combine the water, pork bones, back fat and pork in a large stock pot. Gradually bring to the boil over a medium heat, skimming the scum off the surface as it begins to bubble. Simmer for about half an hour, or until no new scum rises to the top, skimming constantly. Top up the water to cover the bones and continue to simmer for 3 hours, topping up the water as necessary to keep everything covered.

After 3 hours, add the soy sauce, MSG, mirin, leek, carrot, garlic, ginger and pork joint, and continue to cook, ensuring at this point that the broth is only gently simmering so the chashu doesn't get tough. Simmer for about 1½ hours until the chashu is tender (you'll need to be able to bite through it easily, so make sure it's quite soft), then remove. Pass the broth through a sieve and measure it – you should have about 960 ml (32 fl oz/4 cups) of broth, so boil to reduce the liquid as needed. Taste the reduced broth and add more soy sauce and/or mirin, if you like.

To make the noodles, combine the kansui, salt and water and stir until the salt dissolves. Stir the liquid into the flour in a bowl with a spoon until it forms loose crumbs, then squeeze the crumbs together to form a ball. Cover with a damp cloth and rest for half an hour, then knead the dough with great force – you can either whack the dough with a rolling pin several times, or you can put the dough in a very tough, sturdy plastic bag and stomp on it with your feet (you need to really work the gluten in the dough to give it Jiro's characteristic firm and slippery texture). When the dough has come together, roll it through a pasta roller – at first, it will crumble and be difficult to roll, but the more you pass it through the machine, the more solid and flexible it will become. Keep rolling, folding the dough over itself each time, until it comes out in a solid sheet. Continue to roll, adjusting the roller until the dough is 3 mm (⅛ in) thick. Cut the dough on the linguini 3 mm (⅛ in) attachment and dust the noodles with a little flour to keep them from sticking together.

To serve, bring the broth and large pan of water to the boil. If you're using the back fat as a topping, put it in the broth and let it boil as you prepare the other ingredients. Boil the bean sprouts and cabbage in the broth for about 1 minute, then remove (use a noodle basket or a deep sieve for this). Cook the noodles until tender but still with plenty of bite – since they're thick this will probably take 2–3 minutes. Meanwhile, divide the broth between 2 bowls. Drain the noodles very well and place them in the broth. Top with the bean sprouts, cabbage, chashu, back fat (if using) and garlic.

東
京
ロ
ー
カ
ル

Ramen Jiro's noodles are very distinctive, thickly cut, hard and slightly wavy. It may be difficult to find the right noodles, so I've included a recipe for them here. If it's too much trouble, just get the chunkiest ramen you can.

FUKAGAWA MESHI

RICE WITH CLAMS AND MISO BROTH

Fukagawa is an old working-class neighbourhood of East Tokyo whose name literally means 'deep river' – an evocative descriptor for this dish, characterised by its generous quantity of *asari* clams. The story goes that clams were plentiful and inexpensive in old Edo, so this became a popular, cheap, filling meal for fishermen and merchants who lived among the markets and docks. Though rarely seen in other areas of Japan (or even Tokyo), it remains a neighbourhood favourite, with numerous shops specialising in it around the serene Kiyosumi-Shirakawa area. And it's easy to see why – the meaty clams and rich, savoury broth are enormously comforting, like a kind of *washoku* version of clam chowder.

SERVES 2

100 ml (3½ fl oz/scant ½ cup) sake
½ leek (white part), thinly sliced
10 g (½ oz) ginger root, peeled and finely shredded
200 g (7 oz) shimeji mushrooms, roughly chopped
300 g (10½ oz) fresh small clams such as littleneck, carpetshell, asari or cockles, cleaned
500 ml (17 fl oz/2 cups) dashi
1 tablespoon mirin
1 teaspoon soy sauce
20 g (¾ oz) miso
200 g (7 oz/1 cup) rice
2 egg yolks (optional)
½ sheet of nori, cut into fine shreds (or a couple of pinches of kizami-nori)

METHOD

Bring the sake to a simmer in a pan with a lid. Add the leek, ginger and mushrooms and simmer for a few minutes, then add the clams and place a lid on the pan. Steam for 3 minutes until the clams open. Drain and reserve the liquid, then pick all the meat from the shells along with the bits of veg, and reserve. Add the dashi, mirin and soy sauce to the liquid and measure out 260 ml (9 fl oz/generous 1 cup). Stir the miso into the remaining broth. Cook the rice according to the instructions on page 26, using the measured broth instead of water. When the rice is done, fold in half of the clam meat and veg. Scoop the rice into deep bowls and top with the remaining clams and veg. Top with the egg yolks, if using, and the shredded nori, and serve the miso broth in separate bowls on the side. Serve with a side of Tsukudani (page 109) and various pickles.

東
京
ロ
ー
カ
ル

Where to find

Fukagawa Kamasho 深川釜匠 深川釜匠
Kiyosumi-Shirakawa, 〒135-0021

YANAGAWA NABE

HOTPOT OF POND LOACH OR BEEF WITH BURDOCK AND EGG

98

It's a bit strange to talk about Tokyo's 'natural features', because it hardly has any. Even Tokyo's bays and rivers have been literally bent to the will of the people over the years. But those bays and rivers are still home to a variety of aquatic plants and animals, many of which are edible, if not exactly trophy fish. One of the more readily available critters to be found in Tokyo's waterways is the *dojo*, or pond loach, which look like wriggly little eels but are actually more closely related to carp or catfish. They're a bit like the eels of the Thames – not the most popular of foods due to their wormy appearance and earthy flavour, but iconic nonetheless, and particularly popular among older locals. Dojo can be grilled, like eel, but they're more commonly cooked in a couple different kinds of hotpot called *dozeu nabe* or *yanagawa nabe* – 'dozeu' is a local pronunciation of 'dojo,' while origins of the name 'yanagawa' aren't really understood, but it was probably the name of one of a few different shops that began selling it in the 19th century.

Dozeu nabe is very simply whole dojo boiled in a sweet soy and dashi sauce and topped with spring onions, while Yanagawa nabe is slightly more extravagant; the dojo are deboned and butterflied before cooking, and the dish includes shaved burdock and beaten egg, sometimes garnished with the Japanese herb *mitsuba*. Both dishes do little to disguise the muddy flavour of the dojo, but the good news is, you don't have to make Yanagawa nabe with dojo at all (and at any rate, you probably won't be able to get them; even in Tokyo, they're not common). Yanagawa nabe has since become a catch-all term for any hotpot cooked with a soy sauce and mirin-based broth, burdock and eggs, and is now even made with beef – which is delicious, but you could also do this with other richly flavoured fish instead of the dojo, such as sardines, herring or eel.

SERVES 4

20 dojo (pond loaches), or more likely, 16–20 sardines, deboned and butterflied – or you can use about 400 g (14 oz) cheap lean beef (such as hanger or rump), very thinly sliced
100 ml (3½ fl oz/scant ½ cup) sake
2 tablespoons plus 1 teaspoon rice vinegar
½ burdock root, washed
1 small bunch (about 100 g (3½ oz)) nira, cut into about 3-cm (1-in) pieces
250 ml (8½ fl oz/1 cup) prepared dashi
50 ml (1¾ fl oz/3 tablespoons) soy sauce
1 teaspoon mirin
1 tablespoon caster (superfine) sugar
4 eggs
shichimi, to taste

METHOD

If you're using the dojo or sardines, toss them in half the sake and leave to soak for about half an hour. Rinse the sake off with plenty of cold running water, and leave to drain well. Have a bowl of fresh water ready with 2 tablespoons of vinegar added to it. Peel the burdock root and cut it into fine shavings – the Japanese technique for this is to hold the knife blade away from you and cut the root as if you were whittling a spear or sharpening a pencil. Place the shavings in the vinegared water to prevent them from discolouring.

Place the dashi in a hotpot or flameproof casserole and bring to a simmer. Add the remaining 50 ml (1¾ fl oz/3 tablespoons) of sake, 1 teaspoon of vinegar, soy sauce, mirin and sugar. Add the shaved burdock, place a lid on the pan and cook for about 5 minutes until the burdock is tender, then add the dojo/sardines/beef, place the lid back on the pan, and cook for another 5 minutes. Add the nira and then the eggs, break their yolks into the broth and mix them slightly. Sprinkle with shichimi and serve with bowls of rice.

東京ローカル

Where to find
Iidaya 飯田屋
Asakusa, 〒111-0035, asakusa-ryoin.jp/iidaya/

AGEMANJU

TEMPURA-FRIED, FILLED SWEET DUMPLINGS

100

There's a place in Asakusa called Nakamise Dori, a shopping street leading up to the famous Kaminarimon gate at Senso-Ji temple, which is absolutely the most shamefully touristy street in Tokyo. It's always heaving with slack-jawed out-of-towners, both from abroad and from elsewhere in Japan, and most of the shops sell hideously garish 'wacky Japanese' souvenirs such as Godzilla figurines, cheap plastic lucky cats, bargain-bin kimonos, and headbands and t-shirts that say obnoxious things like 'foreign devil' or 'looking for a Japanese girlfriend'. But there are some diamonds in the rough down Nakamise Dori: a wonderful handmade chopstick boutique; a shop selling vintage Japanese prints; a place that makes beautiful fans from Japanese paper and prints; and a stall at the very end selling *agemanju*, a kind of sweet filled dumpling fried in a light tempura batter. Grab one of these, hot from the fryer, and a bottle of ramune from the stall next door, and just stand and gawk at Kaminarimon's famous red lantern while you enjoy your snack and smell the incense wafting over the temple. It may be touristy and it may be trashy but to me it's an essential Tokyo experience.

This recipe is for agemanju filled with sweet red bean paste, but you can do it with all kinds of other fillings – sweetened *kabocha* squash is one of my favourites. Ideally, use a probe thermometer for this recipe.

MAKES 8 DUMPLINGS

For the dough
80 ml (3 fl oz/⅓ cup) milk
200 g (7 oz/scant 1⅔ cups) plain (all-purpose) flour
2 tablespoons caster (superfine) sugar
1 teaspoon baking powder
1 teaspoon vegetable oil
500 g (1 lb 2 oz) sweet red bean paste

For the batter
80 g (3 oz/⅔ cup) plain (all-purpose) flour
20 g (¾ oz) cornflour (cornstarch) or potato starch
1 teaspoon baking powder
pinch of salt
90 ml (3 fl oz/⅓ cup) cold sparkling water
oil, for deep-frying

METHOD

Stir together the milk, plain flour, sugar, baking powder and vegetable oil until a soft dough forms. Knead it a few times, then divide into 8 pieces and roll each piece out into a round about 9 cm (3½ in) in diameter. Place a big spoonful of bean paste in the centre of each round, then gather the dough around the paste and pinch to seal. Refrigerate for at least 30 minutes. Meanwhile, whisk together the plain flour, cornflour or potato starch, baking powder and salt, then mix in the sparkling water – keep the batter slightly lumpy, which will help make the crust light and lacy.

Heat the oil to 180°C (350°F). If you don't have a thermometer, simply drip a few drops of the batter into the oil to test it. If the batter sinks, it's too cold. If the batter immediately floats and sizzles, it's too hot. If the batter sinks just below the surface of the oil, then rises up and start to sizzle, it should be perfect. Dip the bean dumplings in the batter, then deep-fry for about 6 minutes, turning the dumplings over once during cooking, until the crust is hard and pale golden in colour. Drain on paper towels and eat piping hot.

東
京
ロ
ー
カ
ル

Where to find
Asakusa Kokonoe 浅草九重
Asakusa, 〒111-0032, agemanju.jp

FUKUJIN PICKLES

SWEET AND SALTY SEVEN-VEGETABLE PICKLES

The jammy, sweet flavour of these pickles makes them almost like a kind of Japanese chutney – which is perhaps why they're most often found alongside a big plate of curry rice. They are indeed a rather perfect partner – crunchy and mild to counter Japanese curry's softness and spice. The name 'Fukujin' refers to the 'Seven Lucky Gods' of Japanese mythology, and there are a few stories that explain how these simple pickles got their name. But my favourite one says that the Edo period satirist Baitei Kinga deemed the pickles so flavourful and satisfying that even to eat them with just a bowl of rice and nothing else would make one feel wealthy – as if the Seven Lucky Gods had paid a visit. But really, it's more likely that the name comes from one of the shops or temples in Tokyo that first started selling it, or it may be simply a fanciful reference to the traditional inclusion of seven key ingredients: daikon, aubergine, cucumber, sword beans, lotus root, shiso and shiitake.

Fukujin zuke are commonly dyed red, either from purple shiso leaves, beetroot, or artificial colourings. Feel free to add any of these if you like, but for me they are unnecessary.

½ aubergine (eggplant), cut lengthways
5-cm (2-in) chunk of lotus root, peeled
½ cucumber
100 g (3½ oz) daikon, peeled
50 g (2 oz) shiitake, destemmed
50 g (2 oz) mangetout (snow peas)
salt
10 shiso leaves (purple if you can get them),
    roughly torn
100 ml (3½ fl oz/scant ½ cup) soy sauce
80 ml (3 fl oz/⅓ cup) sake
1 tablespoon rice vinegar
1 tablespoon mirin
1 teaspoon caster (superfine) sugar
1 teaspoon white sesame seeds

METHOD

Cut the aubergine in half lengthways so you have two long triangular prisms. Cut the lotus root, cucumber and daikon in half as well to make semi-circles. Slice all the veg except the mangetout thinly, about 2–3 mm (⅛ in) thick (you may want to use a mandoline if you have one). Cut the mangetout in half widthways.

Salt the sliced veg generously and mix them in a bowl, then leave to sit for about half an hour – they should have wilted and become pliable. Rinse the vegetables under cold running water until they no longer taste salty. Place the shiso, soy sauce, sake, vinegar, mirin, sugar and sesame seeds in a saucepan and bring to the boil. Add the veg and boil until the liquid reduces to a very thick glaze, stirring frequently – this should be a very quick cook so the veg retain their crunch. Remove from the pan and chill well before serving.

103

YAKITORI

GRILLED CHICKEN

104

I've often thought about offering olfactory tours of different cities. In London, for example, you could mosey around Chinatown, sniffing the likes of heady five-spice-braised meats, pungent Sichuan hotpot broths, and fresh, buttery Cantonese cakes. In Los Angeles you could enjoy the aromas of chilli and charcoal from Korean barbecue joints, lard and limes from taco trucks and, of course, the omnipresent exhaust fumes of LA traffic. In Tokyo, you could smell all kinds of things, but perhaps most commonly, the bittersweet smoke of *yakitori*, which seems to billow out from just about every back street.

Yakitori is humble, casual food, no doubt, but nevertheless there is a certain level of craftsmanship that goes into it, varying from perfunctory to perfectionist. Like sushi, yakitori is more about technique than it is about specific recipes, so what follows is a general guide to grilling a few typical yakitori preparations, with a few suggestions for seasonings. Yakitori can be done well enough under the grill, but to me there's little point to it unless you're doing it over charcoal – the smoke and char is a key part of the flavour. But it's quite easy to construct a makeshift yakitori set-up at home – all you need is two rows of bricks set over hot coals, spaced apart in such a way that you can rest either end of your skewers on the bricks with the meat hanging over the heat. As with all barbecuing, you'll need hot and cold zones in the coals to regulate the cooking so certain cuts of chicken don't burn before they're cooked through; you can achieve this by simply piling the coals deeper on one side, or moving cooler embers over to one side while periodically adding more fresh coals to the other.

A FEW KEY TYPES OF YAKITORI TO TRY:

NEGIMA

Chunks of chicken thigh interwoven with chunks of spring onion (scallion), cut to a similar size. I actually prefer to use baby leeks for this, because the spring onions in the UK tend to be a bit too scrawny and hollow to make for a satisfying skewer. Keep these on the colder part of the grill to soften the onions and cook the thighs through before moving them to the hot side to crisp their skin and char the onions.

TSUKUNE

Chicken meatballs or patties. These are best when they're made from coarsely minced (ground) chicken (often hand-ground by cleaver) and flavoured with lots of garlic, ginger, white pepper and spring onions (scallions). Some *tsukune* use binders like potato starch or egg, but I think these are unnecessary and also yield an inferior texture. Simply mince (grind) the chicken (leg meat works best but you can also incorporate whatever bits of meat you can scrape from the carcass) just enough so that it holds together, then shape it into balls or logs around the skewers. Cook these over medium-hot coals.

OYSTERS

This often overlooked nugget of pure chicken joy makes for one of the most effortlessly delicious skewers. A lazy muscle that just sort of hangs out at the back of the bird above the top thigh joint, the oyster is supremely juicy and flavourful, so cook it over a high heat to crisp the skin and you're good to go. There are only two of them on each bird, so if you're prepping yakitori from a whole chicken, hide these from sight to save them for yourself, or for someone you really love.

HEART

Chicken hearts are full of strong dark meat flavour, but they aren't as rich as other chicken offal because they're a hard-working muscle. This makes them best suited to quick, hot cooking so the outside chars while the inside stays slightly pink and tender.

東
京
ロ
ー
カ
ル

Where to find
Tori-shiki 鳥しき
Meguro, 〒141-0021

LIVER

Strongly flavoured and extremely rich, these are also best suited to cooking over very hot coals so they char on the outside without becoming dry in the middle. Trim them of any sinew and pair them with strong, tangy condiments like sweet soy sauce, grated ginger, *yuzu-kosho* or umeboshi.

TEBASAKI/TEBAMOTO

One of the most delicious cuts, chicken wings given the yakitori treatment are like the whole bird in microcosm, incorporating fat, skin, white meat, dark meat and cartilage. Typically, only the two 'prime' joints of the wing – the meatiest ones, not the wingtip – are used. *Tebasaki* is the middle joint, while *tebamoto* is the shoulder joint or drumstick. These are woven onto two skewers to spread out their skin, then cooked over a medium-low heat to tenderise the connective tissues as the skin slowly crisps.

BONJIRI

The tail, or 'parson's nose', of the bird is strictly for those with a taste for chicken fat, because that makes up the bulk of it; *bonjiri* also contains a little bone and cartilage, which you can chomp right through, or delicately gnaw around. These should be cooked over a medium-low heat to crisp the skin without burning it.

SKIN

Chicken skin makes amazing yakitori, but it requires a deft hand on the grill; you have to render off the fat and moisture from the skin without burning it, which is quite tricky because it produces a lot of flare-ups as the fat drips onto the coals below. It's a cheat, but I always pre-render the chicken skin in either an oven or a frying pan (skillet) set over a low heat to get most of the fat and water out before threading it onto skewers and grilling. Then it's a matter of placing it over a medium-low heat, turning frequently, until it becomes golden brown, crisp on the outside and still juicy on the inside.

Once you've decided on what sort of yakitori to prepare, you have to choose a seasoning. Usually there are two options: a sweet soy-based sauce called *tare*, or just salt. Which you choose is up to you, but most people go for the tare with more richly flavoured, meaty cuts like liver, thigh and tsukune,

while salt is used for cuts that already have a leaner, sweeter flavour, like fillet, wings or hearts. But really the choice is yours. By the way, if you are using salt, I highly recommend you use what's called 'flavour salt' in Japan: MSG. MSG is a superior seasoning to enhance the flavour of the bird as it draws out its sweetness and umami (and it's completely harmless, in case you haven't heard). I also like salted yakitori with plenty of finely ground white pepper and a tiny bit of lemon.

The following is a very basic recipe for yakitori tare, but you can adjust it however you like – make it saltier with more soy sauce, thicker with cornflour or potato starch, sweet with sugar, lighter with sake, or more tangy with vinegar. It is more common to make tare with mirin, but I prefer honey because it's thicker and has such a nice aroma.

ALL-PURPOSE YAKITORI TARE

THIS WILL BE ENOUGH
FOR ABOUT 12-15 SKEWERS

3 tablespoons caster (superfine) sugar
1 tablespoon honey
3 tablespoons sake
1 tablespoon soy sauce
1 tablespoon tonkatsu sauce or ketchup
¼ teaspoon dashi powder
¼ teaspoon pepper

METHOD

Place the sugar and honey in a small saucepan and cook over a medium-low heat until the sugar melts and the mixture begins to caramelise. Add the sake and soy sauce and bring to the boil, stirring to dissolve the sugar. Then add the tonkatsu sauce, dashi powder and pepper. Continue to cook over a medium heat until the mixture thickens to the consistency of a thin syrup.

TONKATSU

FRIED PORK CHOP

Tonkatsu is mainly associated with areas of Japan known for their pork, like Kagoshima, but Tokyo is nevertheless one of the best places in the country to try this quintessential *yoshoku* dish. Tonkatsu chefs in Tokyo can be as obsessive as sushi chefs, going to great lengths to ensure every element of this über-schnitzel is perfect: the pork, the panko, the oil, the sauces and garnishes, and even the flour and eggs used for panéing are chosen with care, and the results can often be spectacular.

All tonkatsu recipes are basically the same – pork, breadcrumbs, frying – so making a good one really is about selecting the best possible ingredients, and cooking them with care. Most tonkatsu is available in two different cuts: fillet (tenderloin) or loin. Either way, you need to use really good pork. Choose a breed known for flavour and marbling, such as Berkshire, Kurobuta, Tamworth, Mangalitza or Duroc. Whatever you choose, make sure the meat is red or deep pink (not pale pink and definitely not white) and has a lot of fat throughout the muscle. Some butchers now sell aged pork, which will provide excellent flavour and tenderness.

The flour should be strong bread flour, which makes a better adhesive than plain flour, and the panko is important as well. I like panko that's in really long shards but not chunky – big thick panko will be hard and dense, while longer, thinner panko come out light and delicately crisp. The oil should be clean and neutral, like sunflower or rapeseed (canola).

And then it is all about the cooking. Many recipes recommend frying the tonkatsu in oil kept below 100°C (212°F), and then finishing it at a high temperature for colour and crunch. I understand the reasoning behind this (lower, slower cooking means less moisture is lost via evaporation, and the meat will stay more juicy and tender if it's not overcooked), but frying at a low temperature tends to make the panko absorb more oil. Always remember that underdone meat can be cooked more – but overdone meat is irrevocable. Err on the side of rare, and also bear in mind that despite what your mother may have told you, pork is perfectly safe to eat (and also really delicious) if it's still a bit pink.

While researching tonkatsu restaurants in Tokyo I came across a review of a place called Tonta in Takadanobaba that said the tonkatsu there is so good that it doesn't need sauce. This is perhaps the best benchmark to try to reach when making tonkatsu. (Then again, tonkatsu sauce is delicious.)

You will need a probe thermometer.

MAKES 2 CUTLETS

400 g (14 oz) really good-quality, well-marbled, skinless and boneless pork loin, cut into two cutlets a minimum of 2 cm (¾ in) thick
salt, as needed
1 egg
1 tablespoon vegetable oil, plus more for deep-frying
about 25 g (1 oz/2 tablespoons) strong white bread flour, as needed
150 g (5 oz/12½ cups) light, long, good-quality panko (or more, as needed)
¼ hispi or similar sweet cabbage, finely shredded
tonkatsu sauce (optional)

METHOD

Season each cutlet liberally with salt and rub it into the meat. If you have time, leave the pork to rest for an hour (or overnight) so the salt can really permeate the meat. Beat the egg with the vegetable oil – this helps create a watertight barrier around the meat, trapping in moisture. Dredge the cutlets in the flour, and then dunk in the egg mixture. Leave the pork in the egg for a few minutes so the flour absorbs the egg and forms a kind of glue, then dredge in the panko, ensuring that the cutlet is thoroughly and completely coated. Heat the oil to 160°C (320°F), then lower the pork into it and cook for about 5–6 minutes. Probe the centre of the meat – when it is about 60°C (140°F), remove from the heat, drain on paper towel, and leave to rest on a wire rack for at least 5 minutes. Slice into chopstick-friendly pieces. Serve with the cabbage and tonkatsu sauce, if you like.

東京ローカル

Where to find
Butagumi 豚組
Roppongi, 〒106-0031, butagumi.com

TSUKUDANI

SEAWEED PRESERVED IN SWEET SOY SAUCE

Tsukudani is one of those fantastic Japanese condiments that delivers maximum flavour out of humble ingredients, the kind of thing that you only need a little spoonful of to season a whole bowl of rice. Another old Edo speciality with its roots in the fishing communities around Tokyo Bay, tsukudani is named for Tsukuda Island, where fishermen began preserving sea vegetables and small sea animals to eat with rice while out on their boats, or to have something to eat and sell when inclement weather made for poor catches. Their hardships are our gain, because tsukudani is delicious: incredibly sweet, salty, fishy and umami, perfect as onigiri filling (page 46) or as a little side dish to have with other snacks and beer or sake.

Common tsukudani ingredients include dried baby sardines, baby eels, little clams, mushrooms, wakame and, in some regions, locusts or bee larvae, but this recipe is for a basic one using spent kombu and katsuobushi from making Dashi (page 184). But feel free to use whatever you like – the method is the same regardless.

MAKES ENOUGH FOR ABOUT 4 ONIGIRI/BOWLS OF RICE/LITTLE SIDE DISHES

rehydrated kombu and katsuobushi from
    making Dashi (page 184)
150 ml (5 fl oz/scant ⅔ cup) water
1 tablespoon caster (superfine) sugar
1 tablespoon soy sauce
1 teaspoon mirin
1 teaspoon rice vinegar
1 teaspoon sake
2 teaspoons dashi powder
10–12 leaves shiso, roughly chopped, or 2 teaspoons
    yukari (shiso-flavoured furikake)
2 teaspoons white sesame seeds

METHOD

Julienne the kombu into fine shreds, and coarsely chop the katsuobushi. Place in a saucepan with the water, sugar, soy sauce, mirin, vinegar, sake and dashi powder and bring to the boil. Continue to cook until the liquid reduces to a very thick glaze. This could take anything from 20 to 40 minutes so lower the heat at this point to prevent it from burning and keep stirring regularly. Then stir in the shiso or yukari and white sesame. Continue to cook, whilst stirring frequently, until the liquid has reduced to a very thick glaze that is the consistency of honey. Leave to cool completely before using.

東
京
ロ
ー
カ
ル

TOKYO N

2

DARUMA 達磨

TAKO たこ

ATIONAL

TAKOYAKI タコヤキ

2F

TOKYO NATIONAL

JAPANESE REGIONAL CUISINE
IN THE CAPITAL

One of my favourite things about travelling in Japan is trying the local specialities; every region, every prefecture, every big city and every tiny town seems to have at least one thing they're famous for, whether it's a strange sea creature, delightful local hooch, or a biscuit with President Obama's face on it (Google it).

Tokyo isn't really known for its local food, mainly because it doesn't need to be: instead of a few specific things, it has some of everything. And that includes foods it has drawn in from other parts of Japan. While visiting Tokyo alone will never be the same as a full tour of the archipelago, it is possible to try all sorts of regional dishes there, including dishes from the furthest-flung peripheries of Japan, like Okinawa. Some of this food is exceedingly rare outside of its place of origin, so it's definitely worth seeking out if you're after a taste of some of Japan's deeper culinary cuts. Take a tour of Japan without ever leaving Tokyo!

MIYAZAKI-STYLE YUZU-KOSHO

SALTED CITRUS-CHILLI PASTE

114

Some regional Japanese specialties can be found in Tokyo restaurants, but others you're more likely to come across in shops. Like the wine and cheese of France, produce from certain areas of Japan can become so well known and highly regarded that the region itself becomes a kind of brand name. One such region is Miyazaki, a prefecture in Kyushu that is famous for (among other things) shochu, chicken and tropical fruits. Miyazaki food is so popular, in fact, that the prefectural government has set up a Miyazaki grocery store in Shinjuku. You'll find all sorts of delicious and obscure items there, including a wide range of *yuzu-kosho*, the condiment made by pounding chillies and yuzu peel together with salt. This pungent paste is not particularly well known outside of Japan, but it does have a sort of cult following among UK chefs and foodies. And it's an easy thing to love – preserving the peel of yuzu with salt is one of the best ways to capture its unique aroma, while the chillies add another layer of complexity, calling to mind coriander (cilantro). The salt and spice in yuzu-kosho makes the flavour extremely potent, and you only need a tiny dab to flavour a bowl of ramen or a hotpot. Stirred through mayonnaise, it also makes a fantastic all-purpose dip.

Yuzu-kosho is available at any Japanese supermarket, but it's easy to make from scratch, and if you make it yourself you can adjust the flavour however you like. At my restaurant we make ours from Scotch bonnet chillies, which makes it super-spicy and incredibly fruity. But I've also made a chilli-free yuzu paste that I called 'yuzu-nosho', which delivers maximum yuzu flavour without any heat. So play around with this recipe and make it your own. Also, if you can't get yuzu peel, you can make this with just about any other citrus instead, which is a great way to eliminate a bit of wastage from your kitchen – just save your lime/lemon/grapefruit/orange peels, trim them of their white pith, then proceed with the recipe with those instead of yuzu.

MAKES ABOUT A 150 ML (5 FL OZ) JAR

100 g (3½ oz) yuzu peel, trimmed of white pith (you can use frozen yuzu peel for this if you can't get the fresh fruit, but not dried), coarsely chopped
8 g (¼ oz) chilli, coarsely chopped (start with something not too spicy, like jalapeño, with the seeds in and, if you decide you want it spicier, you can move onto more intense chillies like serrano, finger chillies, bird's eye or habanero)
6 g (¼ oz) salt

METHOD

Combine the yuzu peel, chilli and salt in a bowl and mix well. Leave to sit for half an hour for the salt to permeate and soften the fruit. Transfer to a mortar or a food processor and pound/grind/process to a paste (it should be fairly smooth; some chunks are ok but they shouldn't be too big). Pack into a jar and press cling film (plastic wrap) onto the surface of the paste (if it is exposed to air it can spoil). Cover and leave at room temperature for one week to ferment; the yuzu-kosho is ready to use when the colour darkens and the flavour becomes noticeably more mellow, tangy and sweet. Keep in the fridge for up to 3 months.

東京で全国

SAPPORO-STYLE BUTTER CORN MISO RAMEN

116

Tokyo is fantastic for ramen, no doubt (see Harukiya-style Old-School Tokyo Shoyu Ramen, page 87, Taishoken-style Tsukemen, page 90, Jiro-Style Ramen, page 95, and Lemon Shio Ramen, page 239, for more). But ramen is one of the most diversified dishes in Japanese gastronomy, and if you're a real ramenhead you will want to seek out some from outside the capital, such as the OG tonkotsu from Kurume, the fat and wavy noodles from Kitakata, or the heavily Taiwanese-inflected versions found in Nagoya. Luckily, many of Japan's 'greatest hits' of ramen are actually well represented in Tokyo itself, and one in particular I'd recommend trying is miso ramen from Sapporo, topped with butter and corn. Butter and corn may sound odd, but they're both long-established products of Hokkaido, where northern European-style agriculture has been practised since the late 19th century. But more important than their history is their flavour; butter and sweetcorn are perfect complements to miso ramen, providing a lovely sweetness and texture to accent the tangy broth and chewy noodles.

SERVES 4

For the broth
1.2 litres (40 fl oz/4¾ cups) unseasoned, good-quality chicken or pork broth (please not from a stock cube – if you're making broth from scratch, try the recipes on pages 87, 95 or 239)
10 g (½ oz) dried mushrooms (shiitake, porcini or really any kind will do), washed if necessary
80 g (3 oz) miso (use red miso or barley miso if you can get it)

For the meat
8 spring onions (scallions)
2 tablespoons oil, plus more as needed
4 garlic cloves, thinly sliced
190–200 g (7 oz/small) tin of sweetcorn, drained
250 g (9 oz) very fatty minced (ground) pork
½ tablespoon white sesame seeds, toasted until deep golden brown
¼ teaspoon black or white pepper
40 g (1½ oz) miso

For the toppings
¼ hispi or similar sweet cabbage, core removed and roughly chopped
150 g (5 oz) bean sprouts
2 teaspoon sesame oil
4 portions wavy, medium-thick ramen noodles (instant is good; dried is better; fresh is best)
8 slices of Chashu (page 87)
50–60 g (2 oz) butter, cut into 4 pats

東京で全国

Where to find
Ramen Kitanodaichi ラーメン北の大地 Shinjuku, 〒 160-0022, ramen-kitanodaichi.jp

METHOD

Combine the broth and mushrooms and bring to a simmer. Leave the mushrooms to infuse into the broth for 10 minutes, then remove with a slotted spoon, pressing or squeezing them out as you do. Add the miso to the pan and whisk to dissolve. Roughly chop the rehydrated mushrooms. Keep the broth at a low simmer until ready to use.

Finely slice the green parts of the spring onions at an angle and set aside, then coarsely chop the white parts. Pour the oil in a frying pan (skillet) and add the garlic slices, then set on a medium-low heat and let the garlic slowly fry until it is golden in colour and crispy (don't let the oil get too hot or the garlic will burn before it goes crisp – take your time with it). Remove the garlic from the oil with a slotted spoon and drain on paper towels. Return the pan to a medium-high heat and add the sweetcorn. Sauté until browned, then remove with a slotted spoon and set aside. If the pan is dry at this point, add a little more oil, return to a high heat, add the white spring onions and fry until they begin to colour. Add the pork, sesame seeds, pepper, miso and chopped mushrooms and stir-fry for something like 10 minutes until the pork is cooked through and slightly browned, making sure to break up any big chunks of meat or miso as you go. Remove from the heat.

Meanwhile, bring about 2 litres (70 fl oz/8 cups) of water to the boil in a separate saucepan. Blanch the cabbage and bean sprouts in the boiling water for 30–60 seconds, then remove with a slotted spoon or sieve, transfer to a bowl, and toss with the sesame oil. Cook the noodles in the water according to the packet instructions – this should be no more than 5 minutes and probably much less, depending on the manufacturer. While the noodles are cooking, stir the miso-chicken broth before ladling it into deep bowls. Drain the noodles and place them in the hot broth, then top with the pork, cabbage and bean sprouts, green spring onions, sweetcorn, garlic chips, chashu, and finally, the butter just before serving so it doesn't fully melt before it gets to the table. Enjoy piping hot with a cold Sapporo beer.

東
京
で
全
国

KAGAWA-STYLE UDON

118

Udon is enjoyed all over Japan, but for some reason it seems to have fewer regional variations compared to other noodle dishes like ramen. This could be because it is considered a more 'traditional' food, and therefore subject to narrower parameters in terms of method and customer expectations, or it could be because one regional udon is simply so popular that it has completely dominated udon culture not only in Japan, but around the world: *Kagawa udon*.

Kagawa is a prefecture in Shikoku, the smallest and least populous of Japan's four major islands. Kagawa udon is perhaps more frequently called *Sanuki udon*, invoking Kagawa's ancient provincial name along with its traditional produce that supposedly make the udon so special: good-quality wheat, sea salt, soy sauce and dried sardines. And these key ingredients do indeed make for damn good udon, which at its best should have a light-yet-satisfying quality, with a broth that's clear and thin but full of umami, and noodles that are strong and thick but also smooth and supple. Whereas ramen has a springy bounce and soba have a clean-breaking brittleness, udon is said to have 'koshi', or strength – a toothsome doughiness that comes from lots of kneading, traditionally done by stomping on it with one's feet. And if you have a sturdy, clean vinyl bag handy, give that a go – it's actually one of the easiest ways to work the gluten in the dough. Otherwise you can use a stand mixer, or punch the dough repeatedly with your fists, which is a great way to vent any righteous anger you may have built up inside of you.

SERVES 4

For the dough
15 g (½ oz) salt
180 ml (6½ fl oz/¾ cup) lukewarm water
300 g (10½ oz/2½ cups) good-quality, finely ground plain (all-purpose) flour (such as type 00 pasta flour), plus extra for dusting
100 g (3½ oz/heaped ¾ cup) strong bread flour

For the broth
800 ml (28 fl oz/3½ cups) water (soft water is best, if you're being fancy or if you have guests from Shikoku to impress)
20 g (¾ oz) kombu, about a 10-cm (4-in) square, rinsed
20 g (¾ oz) niboshi or iriko, heads and guts removed (prepared weight)
10 g (½ oz) dried shiitake (optional)
10 g (½ oz) katsuobushi
2 tablespoons soy sauce (use usukuchi, if you can)
1 tablespoon mirin
sea salt flakes, to taste

For the toppings
traditional toppings include umbeboshi; fried tofu; nori, wakame and other seaweeds; raw or poached eggs; shichimi; shaved burdock; and fish cakes, such as kamaboko
modern Sanuki udon features just about anything you can think of, including butter, mentaiko and tempera-fried bacon and eggs

東
京
で
全
国

5F
4F
3F
2F
1F
B1F
B2F

119

METHOD

Stir the salt into the water until it dissolves. Combine the salted water and flours using a wooden spoon or a stand mixer with a dough hook. When the dough comes together into a solid, smooth piece, cover with cling film (plastic wrap) and transfer to the fridge for at least 3 hours, or preferably overnight. Remove the dough and knead it, either by hand, hard, for about 10 minutes, folding the dough over itself repeatedly, or in a stand mixer on high speed for 5 minutes, or do it by foot: place the dough in a sturdy plastic bag and stomp on it until it flattens out into a broad sheet, then fold it over itself twice and repeat the process 4 times (this method is both quick and fun, but please ensure hygiene standards are maintained). Once the dough is sufficiently kneaded – at this point it should be very smooth and elastic – leave it to rest at room temperature for 20 minutes.

Dust your work surface generously with flour and roll the dough out to a thickness of about 5 mm (¼ in). Dust the rolled-out dough with more flour and fold the dough into 3 layers. Cut the dough into square noodles with a big, flat-edged knife and dust them with more flour to prevent them from sticking together. The noodles should be cut very soon before you cook them to preserve their texture.

To make the broth, combine the water, kombu, niboshi and shiitake, if using, in a saucepan and slowly bring to a simmer over a low heat. When the water barely starts to bubble, remove from the heat and add the katsuobushi. Leave to infuse for at least half an hour, then pass through a sieve and add the soy sauce and mirin. Taste and add salt to your liking.

To serve, have the broth hot and ready, and prepare a very large pot full of boiling water. Cook the udon in the water, keeping the water at a low boil/high simmer so it cooks more evenly. Because the noodles are thick and strong, they will take a while to cook – check them after 5 minutes (they should be tender but have a bit of chew to them), but they may take more like 10 or even 15 minutes, depending on your preference. When the noodles are done, drain and rinse them well under cool running water to remove excess starch and halt the cooking. Place the noodles into deep bowls and ladle over the hot broth. Add toppings of your choice and serve immediately.

東京で全国

Tokyo National

OSAKA-STYLE TAKOYAKI

OCTOPUS BALLS

122

Although Tokyo is rightly praised outside of the country for its quality and diversity of food, in Japan it's Osaka that's more associated with dining out. One of its nicknames is 'the nation's kitchen' and its unofficial mantra is '*kuidaore*' – eat till you collapse. And Osaka does indeed hold its own in terms of food, with several specialities that have become so popular they can now be found all over Japan. One of these is *takoyaki*, spherical octopus dumplings topped with the always-delicious combination of mayo, Japanese brown sauce, aonori, katsuobushi and pickled ginger. In Tokyo these are commonly found at standing bars that also pour draft whisky highballs, which may be my all-time favourite food and drink pairing, and the best karaoke fuel imaginable. I could literally just stand and eat takoyaki and drink highballs all day, every day. This is how I imagine retirement will be.

Takoyaki requires the use of a special pan but, if you don't have one, and don't want to buy one, you can approximate the process using a non-stick cake pop tin or mini muffin tin, as per the instructions below.

MAKES ABOUT 36 BALLS, ENOUGH
FOR 2-4 PEOPLE (OR ONE PERSON,
IF THAT PERSON IS ME)

1 egg, beaten
350 ml (12¼ fl oz/1½ cups) cold water
1 teaspoon dashi powder
1 teaspoon soy sauce
100 g (3½ oz/heaped ¾ cup) plain (all-purpose) flour
pinch of white pepper
¼ teaspoon baking powder
80 g (3 oz) hispi or flat cabbage, finely chopped
6 spring onions (scallions), thinly sliced
30 g (1 oz) beni shoga, finely chopped
a little oil
200 g (7 oz) cooked octopus, cut into 36 small pieces

To serve
about 180 ml (6½ fl oz/¾ cup) okonomi sauce or
	takoyaki sauce
about 100 g (3½ oz) Kewpie mayo (page 46)
20 g (¾ oz) beni shoga, chopped
a couple of big pinches of aonori
handful of katsuobushi

METHOD

If you're doing this in a cake or muffin pan, preheat the oven to 240°C (475°F/gas 9) and use paper towels to spread a bit of oil on the inside of each mould.

If you are using the cake pan, set it inside the hot oven to heat up for 5–10 minutes.

Combine the egg, water, dashi powder and soy sauce in a bowl and beat well. Add the flour, pepper, baking powder, cabbage, half the spring onions and the beni shoga and stir to form a thin batter.

If you're using a takoyaki pan, set it over a medium-high heat and add a little oil to each hole. For either method, the cooking technique is the same, but timings will be a bit different. Start off by pouring enough batter into the pan to fill the holes (they should overflow a bit, so the surface of the pan around the holes has some batter on them as well). Place a chunk of octopus into each hole. After a few minutes, the bottoms will have cooked and solidified; use chopsticks or wooden skewers to gather the cooked dough into each hole, and turn the cooked bottoms of each dumpling upwards so they are exposed but not quite upside-down.

Add a little more batter to fill up each hole again and continue to cook for a few minutes, then flip the dumplings again so the part that was originally on the bottom is now on the top. Continue to cook for several minutes, turning frequently, so they are golden brown all over. (If you are doing this in the oven you will have to be a bit patient, because every time you open the oven door, the temperature of the pan will drop significantly.) When cooked, the interior of the takoyaki should still be semi-liquid, like a croquette. Remove the takoyaki from the pan and garnish with the sauce, mayo, beni shoga, aonori, remaining spring onions and katsuobushi. Leave to cool slightly before eating.

東京で全国

Where to find
Osaka-ya 大阪屋
Shimokitazawa, 〒155-0031

HIROSHIMA-STYLE OKONOMIYAKI

LAYERED PANCAKE OF NOODLES AND VEGETABLES

124

Okonomiyaki, the savoury pancake filled with ingredients of the customer's choosing, is mostly associated with Osaka, to the endless ire of people from Hiroshima, who have their own unique style of okonomiyaki. The Hiroshima style is sometimes called 'Hiroshima-yaki' to differentiate it, but nothing annoys Hiroshimaites more than this, as in their view, it's the Osaka style that is the inferior knock-off version. I'm not going to get involved in this rivalry, but I will say that Hiroshima okonomiyaki is indeed delicious, especially if you love noodles, like I do. In fact, it's more like layered yakisoba, with noodles, cabbage and toppings griddled separately from the pancake, which takes the form of a thin crêpe that gets draped over everything else. I do like the Osaka style, but it does dominate the okonomiyaki scene in Tokyo, and indeed all of Japan, and the world. So I especially like Hiroshima-style because it's a bit of an okonomiyaki underdog.

This recipe includes sweetcorn, bacon and squid – one of my favourite combinations – but you can leave them out, or add all kinds of other things. You'll need a griddle to make Hiroshima okonomiyaki.

MAKES 2 OKONOMIYAKI, WHICH IS ACTUALLY LIKELY TO BE ENOUGH FOR 4 PEOPLE

100 g (3½ oz/heaped ¾ cup) plain (all-purpose) flour
120 ml (4 fl oz/½ cup) dashi
3 eggs
½ hispi or flat cabbage, finely chopped
100 g (3½ oz) bean sprouts
150–200 g (5–7 oz/small) tin of sweetcorn, drained
4 spring onions (scallions), thinly sliced
about 40 g (1½ oz) beni shoga
vegetable oil
6 rashers streaky bacon
200 g (7 oz) prepared squid, scored and cut into
  1-cm (½-in) wide strips
2 portions fresh yakisoba/egg noodles (or dried
  noodles, parboiled)
about 150 ml (5 fl oz/scant ⅔ cup) okonomi sauce
Kewpie mayo (page 46), as needed
a few pinches of aonori
a few pinches of sesame seeds
handful of katsuobushi

METHOD

Whisk together the flour, dashi and 1 egg to form a thin batter. In a separate bowl, toss together the cabbage, bean sprouts, sweetcorn, half of the spring onions and half of the beni shoga. Set the griddle on medium-high heat and add a little oil, spreading it out into a thin layer with a spatula. Use a ladle to pour out 2 pancakes on the griddle, reserving about a third of the batter in the bowl. Top each pancake with the cabbage mixture, then drizzle the remaining batter of the top of each cabbage pile. Press down on the cabbage pile to flatten it slightly, and cook for about 5 minutes. Top each cabbage pile with 3 rashers of bacon, pressing them down, then deftly flip each pile so the bacon is on the bottom and the pancake is on top. Press everything down again.

Stir-fry the squid in a separate space on the griddle and add the noodles on top of the squid. Toss them together with about a third of the okonomi sauce, then gather them into a circle the same diameter as each pancake. Transfer the pancake-cabbage pile to the top of each circle of noodles and cook for another 5 minutes or so (the noodles should be nice and crisp on the bottom). Meanwhile, fry 2 eggs on the griddle – typically the yolk is broken, but I do like a runny yolk on my okonomiyaki. When the eggs are cooked, transfer them to the top of each okonomiyaki, then cover in okonomi sauce, mayo, aonori, sesame seeds, the remaining beni shoga and spring onions and katsuobushi. Enjoy straight from the griddle, if possible.

Where to find
Satchan さっちゃん
Aoyama Itchome, 〒107-0052

FUKUOKA-STYLE HORUMON-YAKI

BARBECUED OFFAL WITH KOREAN CHILLI SAUCE

Fukuoka, the largest city in Kyushu and the sixth largest city in all of Japan, holds a special place in my heart because I lived in nearby Kitakyushu for two years as a young man. I'd wanted to live in Fukuoka because they're famous for tonkotsu ramen (my favourite food), but when I got there I realised that was just one of dozens of Fukuoka specialities that make it, in my opinion, one of the most interesting and delicious places to eat in the world. Fukuoka provides excellent versions of all the Japanese classics, but it's also home to some highly unusual ingredients and dishes, many of which emerged from the region's long history of international trade and emigration. Fukuoka is especially influenced by Korea – in fact, Fukuoka is closer to Seoul, and MUCH closer to Busan (only 214 km (133 miles)), than it is to Tokyo, so Korean culture is well represented there and, in some instances, fully interwoven with local Japanese culture. Mentaiko is an excellent example: a Korean invention of chilli-cured cod's roe that has become so closely associated with Fukuoka that its Korean origins are seldom even recognised.

Another such dish is *yakiniku*, the (slightly) Japanised local version of Korean barbecue. Yakiniku restaurants, which feature all sorts of cuts of pork and beef, are ubiquitous in Fukuoka, as well as in Tokyo, especially around the unofficial 'Koreatown' of Shin-Okubo. And while most yakiniku isn't thought of as a speciality of any particular region, there is one type that is practically synonymous with Fukuoka: horumon-yaki, or grilled guts. Horumon-yaki is a catch-all for pretty much any kind of offal, but most commonly it refers to cuts from the digestive tract, such as stomach or intestines. Pork chitterlings are my favourite variety of offal meat, so that's what this recipe is for, but you can try all manner of guts using the same recipe and technique.

SERVES 2-4

200 g (7 oz) pork chitterlings (small intestines), well cleaned
800 ml (28 fl oz/3½ cups) water, plus more for blanching
50 ml (1¾ fl oz/3 tablespoons) rice vinegar
150 ml (5 fl oz/scant ⅔ cup) sake, plus 100 ml (3½ fl oz/scant ½ cup) sake
4-cm (1½-in) piece of ginger root, thinly sliced (no need to peel)
100 g (3½ oz) gochujang
juice of 2 limes
1 tablespoon caster (superfine) sugar
big pinch of black pepper
a few leaves of cabbage
1–2 stalks nira, thinly sliced
pinch of sesame seeds

METHOD

Cut the chitterlings into rounds about 1 cm (½ in) wide, similar to calamari. Place in a saucepan, cover with cold water and bring to the boil. Drain, discard the water, and rinse the chitterlings well, then return to the pan with the measured water, vinegar, half the sake and the ginger. Bring to the boil and cook for 1½ hours until the chitterlings are tender, remembering to top up the water as needed. Drain the chitterlings and cool.

Meanwhile, stir together the remaining sake, gochujang, lime juice, sugar and black pepper. Toss the chitterlings through this mixture and leave to marinate for about 1 hour. Grill quickly on a mesh set over hot charcoal or on skewers until nicely charred. Garnish with cabbage, nira and sesame.

Where to find

Kura 蔵
Akasaka, 〒107-0052, e-kura.org

東京で全国

OKINAWAN CUISINE

From Tokyo, Okinawa is the furthest-flung region of Japan, which means not many foreign visitors venture there, at least not on their first trip. This is a shame because it is one of the most culturally fascinating parts of the country (and of course it has beautiful beaches). Okinawa was the domain of the Ryukyu people from the 15th to 19th centuries, a distinct ethnic group whose roots were probably a combination of Chinese, Japanese and Micronesian. Ryukyu culture remains distinctive from its neighbours, although both modern and ancient influences from China and Japan can be found there. Since the end of World War II, there has also been a large, persistent and mostly unpleasant American military presence there, which has had an interesting impact on the local food. So the cuisine of Okinawa is unique: a bit Ryukyu, a bit Chinese, a bit Japanese and a bit American, combined into preparations that frequently make use of the islands' unusual local produce.

Luckily, you don't have to jump on a plane to get a taste of Okinawan food and culture; you can do it right in the heart of Tokyo, where a handful of restaurants serve Okinawan dishes and the delicious Okinawan rice spirit *awamori*, often in settings that evoke rustic beachside shacks, with colourful Ryukyu fabrics and live performances. At Okinawa Paradise in Shinjuku, you can try a range of delicious Okinawan dishes and sip awamori while an Okinawan MC croons in the Ryukyu language and strums a three-stringed *shamisen* in between banter with the audience. Go here on your first or second night in Tokyo; the food, drink and island vibes are a brilliant way to blast away your jetlag.

TOFU-YO

Tofu-yo is firm tofu slowly fermented in awamori, along with the live culture used in the fermentation of said awamori. The result is a dense, creamy tofu product, pink in colour with a heady aroma and intense, cheesy flavour. Because of its intensity it is served in very small portions (at Okinawa Paradise we were served a single cube) and eaten in tiny morsels with toothpicks. It requires patience and some obscure ingredients, but your efforts will be rewarded with one of Asia's most delectable drinking snacks. The flavour is truly profound.

MAKES 300 G (10½ OZ), ENOUGH FOR ABOUT 10 SERVINGS

300 g (10½ oz/1 block) firm cotton tofu
200 g (7 oz) dried red koji rice (also sold as red yeast rice or *hong qu mi*)
2 tablespoons salt
200 ml (7 fl oz/scant 1 cup) awamori (or *shochu*), use one that is 20–30% ABV

METHOD

Okinawan tofu is dense and rich, so to replicate it at home you have to dry out a firm tofu. Get very firm cotton tofu and cut it into 3 cm (1 in) cubes, then microwave for 2 minutes to expel excess water. Drain the tofu and microwave again for 2 minutes, then place the tofu on a mesh or perforated tray in an oven set to 60°C (140°F/minimum gas) for 4 hours. The tofu should be very firm and its surface should be dry to the touch.

Combine the dried tofu, red koji rice, salt and awamori in a zip-top bag. Gently shake the bag to mix and dissolve the koji and salt. Seal the bag but leave one corner of the seal open for airflow, then place the bag in a container and leave to ferment at room temperature for at least 2 weeks. The tofu-yo will have developed some flavour by this point, but it will be better if you can leave it for several months! Serve in very small portions with toothpicks to carve off tiny bites.

Where to find Okinawan Cuisine
Okinawa Paradise 沖縄パラダイス
Shinjuku, 〒160-0021

東京で全国

UMIBUDO RICE BOWL

Umibudo, or sea grapes, are a delightful type of sea vegetable famous in Okinawa and, true to their name, they look like bunches of tiny green grapes. (They are also sometimes sold, quite misleadingly, as 'green caviar'.) While they don't have much flavour, they look really cool and have a great texture, popping in the mouth for a fantastic juicy crunch. Amazingly, you can now buy umibudo online and occasionally in shops in the UK, sold dehydrated or in a saltwater brine, but they are rare and astronomically expensive. If you can't get them, or don't want to shell out for them, simply use your favourite edible seaweed instead – samphire is an excellent alternative in terms of flavour and texture.

MAKES 2 RICE BOWLS

3 tablespoons vinegar
3 tablespoons sugar
2 tablespoons soy sauce
2 tablespoons sesame oil
pinch of dashi powder
2 leaves shiso, finely chopped (optional)
2 portions cooked rice (from 150–200 g (5–7 oz/
    ¾–1 cup) uncooked)
200 g (7 oz) sashimi-quality fish of your choice, cut
    into bite-size slices
2 tomatoes, cut into 8 wedges
¼ head iceberg lettuce, roughly torn
100 g (3½ oz) umibudo or similar crunchy vegetable
    (fresh/rehydrated weight)

METHOD

Combine the vinegar, sugar, soy sauce, sesame oil, dashi powder and shiso and stir until the sugar dissolves. To serve, scoop the rice into large bowls, making sure the rice isn't too hot so the lettuce doesn't wilt. Arrange the sashimi, tomatoes and lettuce on top, then add the umibudo. Drizzle the dressing over the dish just before serving.

東京で全国

CHEESY GOYA SPRING ROLLS

Goya, or bitter gourd, can be found all across south and southeast Asia, but in Japan it is strongly associated with Okinawa. Its slightly soapy, bitter flavour can be off-putting at first, but it works well when used to contrast salty, fatty ingredients like Spam or, in this case, melted cheese. This is not a traditional dish as far as I'm aware, but when I had it at Okinawa Paradise I thought it was just too damn good not to include. It also includes another Okinawa speciality, *pochigi* sausage, which is a distant ancestor of Portuguese *linguiça*, which you can use instead, or simply a mild chorizo. With its bitter goya, salty cheese and sausage, and addictive deep-fried crunch, this is possibly the world's greatest drinking food.

MAKES 12 SPRING ROLLS

½ goya (bitter gourd)
salt, as needed
4 spring onions (scallions), finely sliced
120 g (4 oz) linguiça or chorizo, diced
200 g (7 oz) mozzarella or mild Cheddar cheese, grated (or a mix of both)
12 slices of American cheese
12 spring roll wrappers
oil, for deep frying

METHOD

Prepare the goya by scraping out the seeds and as much of the white pith as possible. Cut the goya into a 1 cm (½ in) dice and salt it liberally, then leave to sit for 30 minutes. Rinse the goya under cold running water, then repeat this process once more.

Drain the goya, then combine it with the spring onions, chorizo and grated cheese and mix well. Assemble the rolls one at a time. Wet a spring roll wrapper in a dish of water. Lay a piece of American cheese in the centre, folded over itself, then top with a big spoonful of the goya-chorizo-cheese mixture. Fold the sides of the wrapper over the mound of cheese, then roll up tightly like a burrito. Use a little bit of water on your fingertips to seal the spring roll. Repeat until all the spring rolls are assembled. Ensure the rolls are very well sealed so they don't leak cheese. Heat the oil to 180°C (350°F) and fry the spring rolls for about 6 minutes until golden brown. Drain on paper towel and leave to cool for at least 5 minutes before serving.

東
京
で
全
国

AINU CUISINE

The Ainu are an ethnic group indigenous to Sakhalin and Hokkaido, more closely related to the peoples of Siberia and Mongolia than to the Japanese. The Ainu dominated Hokkaido (formerly Ezo) until the end of the 19th century when the Meiji government began to colonise the island to establish farms, fisheries and factories, forcibly taking Ainu land in the process. Although the Ainu were eventually granted 'aboriginal' status by the government as a token gesture towards the preservation of their culture, in reality they were quickly assimilated into Japanese society. Today, there is no reliable estimate of their numbers, as many Ainu descendants are unaware of their ancestry, so only those who self-identify as Ainu are counted in surveys. In fact, it is not listed as an option on the official Japanese census. The most recent figures estimate the remaining Ainu population to be around 24,000. That's a very small number – and it's dwindling.

As the Ainu people slowly vanish, so do opportunities to learn about their culture first-hand. This hit home for me back in 2007, when I was on holiday in Sapporo. Two years earlier, I had an amazing experience at an Ainu restaurant there while on a research trip. The food was incredible, but what I remember most fondly was the hospitality; the 'restaurant' was really part of an Ainu family's home and their warmth and generosity was genuinely touching; even in a country known for hospitality, theirs stood out. I was the only customer there and they seemed flattered that I wanted to learn about Ainu food; I felt privileged just to have an opportunity to eat it. So when I returned to Sapporo, going back to see them again was at the top of my list of priorities. I didn't have an address, but I remembered the neighbourhood where it was and after an hour of searching I finally found it – permanently closed, and evidently some time ago.

It was one of just three or four Ainu restaurants in the country – now down to just two or three.

One of them is in Tokyo. This is surprising, as the Ainu historically never lived that far south and their cuisine is based on produce local to Hokkaido. But actually I'm thrilled that Tokyo has an Ainu restaurant, because it means more people will have an opportunity to try it; Hokkaido is a great place to visit, but it's too off the beaten track for most tourists to reach. The restaurant, in Okubo, is called Haru Kor – simply meaning 'to have food', but the restaurant is also an unofficial Ainu community and cultural centre, decorated like a traditional thatched house with Ainu textiles and carvings adorning the walls. They hold Ainu spiritual ceremonies for special occasions. And, of course, they serve delicious and totally unique food.

As Ainu culture has merged with Japanese culture, it's sometimes difficult to define what's really traditional and what isn't. But the things that make Ainu cookery distinctive are obvious, mainly because they involve ingredients and techniques virtually unknown in Japanese gastronomy – these include things like Hokkaido-native foraged herbs and vegetables; fish preserved by freezing or drying; and wild game, including venison and bear. The recipes that follow are things you may find on the menu at Haru Kor, and while they may not be exactly what the Ainu were eating hundreds of years ago, they still represent some key flavours from a cuisine that may not even exist much longer, so eat it while you still have the chance.

CHIPORO IMO

MASHED POTATO WITH SALMON ROE

Chiporo imo is an incredibly simple but effective combination of potatoes and salmon roe. The flavour is reminiscient of Russian food, but it's also pure Hokkaido.

SERVES 2

200 g (7 oz) baking potatoes, peeled and cut into
    2.5-cm (1-in) chunks
salt
30 g (1 oz) ikura

METHOD

Boil the potatoes until soft, then drain and mash with a pinch of salt until smooth. Leave to cool, then fold in the ikura.

東
京
で
全
国

Where to find
Haru Kor ハルコロ Shin-Okubo, 〒169-0073

5F
 4F
3F
 2F
1F
B1F
B2F

140

VENISON STIR-FRY, 'GENGHIS KHAN' STYLE

While venison is found in Japanese restaurants – and, in fact – the country has a long history of deer hunting, it is somewhat rare and unusual. But in Ainu cuisine it is considered a delicacy, and features prominently on Haru Kor's menu, as gyoza, sausage, a steak, and in a stir-fry that borrows elements from one of Hokkaido's most popular specialities, 'Ghenghis Khan': griddled lamb with bean sprouts, cabbage and a tangy sauce. Here, the lamb is swapped out for venison and dare I say it is an improvement on the original.

SERVES 2, PERHAPS MORE
IF SERVED WITH RICE AND OTHER SIDES

2 tablespoons soy sauce
2 tablespoons honey
2 tablespoons oyster sauce
1 teaspoon sesame oil
juice of ¼ lemon
1 clove garlic, grated
big pinch white pepper
a little bit of oil
½ onion, thinly sliced
1 small carrot, peeled and julienned
200 g (7 oz) water spinach/morning glory, cut into 5-cm (2-in) pieces
200 g (7 oz) bean sprouts
200–250 g (7–9 oz) good-quality wild venison loin, very thinly sliced

METHOD

Combine the soy sauce, honey, oyster sauce, sesame oil, lemon juice, garlic and white pepper. Stir until well mixed.

Heat the oil in a wok or frying pan over high heat, then add the onion and carrot and stir-fry for a few minutes, until slightly browned. Add the water spinach, bean sprouts and venison, and continue to stir-fry until the venison is just cooked through and the bean sprouts have softened slightly. Add the sauce and continue to stir-fry until everything is well coated.

KITOPIRO CHAHAN

WILD GARLIC FRIED RICE

Kitopiro is a kind of wild allium, sometimes called 'Ainu negi (Ainu onion)' because it is so closely associated with Ainu food. It looks a lot like wild garlic but tastes more like spring onions, both or either of which you can use in its place – tri-cornered leeks, ramps or ramsons would work as well.

SERVES 2 AS A MAIN, 4 AS A SIDE

vegetable oil, for frying
2 eggs
about 50 g (2 oz) wild garlic or similar wild allium, roughly chopped
¼ teaspoon dashi powder
200 g (7 oz/1 cup) rice, cooked and cooled (page 26)
a splash of water
salt and pepper, to taste

METHOD

Heat the oil in a wok or deep frying pan (skillet) over a high heat. Add the eggs and wild garlic and stir-fry for a few minutes until the eggs are cooked through. Add the dashi powder and rice and break it up with your spatula. Add the water and a generous amount of salt and pepper and stir-fry for a few minutes until all the water is gone and the rice is fluffy and tender.

東京で全国

TOKYO

3

GEISHA 芸者

GLOBAL

F

HAMBURGER ハンバーガー

KABUKI 歌舞伎

TOKYO GLOBAL

T
O
K
Y
O

G
L
O
B
A
L

T
O
K
Y
O

G
L
O
B
A
L

FOREIGN-INFLUENCED DELIGHTS

Outside Japan, Tokyo is first and
foremost known for its fantastic
Japanese food. But within Japan,
Tokyo is perhaps better known as
the place with the best foreign food
in the country, with an abundance
of fine German sausage, French
cheese and wine, regional Chinese
specialities, Indian curries,
Peruvian ceviche… hell, you can
even get a nice, handsome pint of
British real ale and fish and chips
in Shinjuku! And while I'd very much
recommend starting with the Japanese
stuff in Tokyo, if you live there, or
have been there a few times, or just
fancy a change of pace from Japanese
cuisine, then it's definitely
worth trying some of the city's
fine foreign (or at least foreign-
influenced) food.

YAKINIKU

KOREAN BARBECUE

148

The carefully cultivated, government-sanctioned image of Japanese food culture is that it's totally monolithic and entirely independent from the culinary traditions of Japan's neighbours. This exceptionalism is preached in particular by proponents of *washoku*, a certain school of officially traditional Japanese food that includes things like *kaiseki*, sushi and *mochi* (as opposed to, say, katsu sando). In 2013, washoku was nominated to UNESCO's Representative List of the Intangible Cultural Heritage of Humanity, indicating that its principles and methods are uniquely worthy of preservation.

It's all bullshit, of course. Japanese culinary traditions are no more distinctive or special than any others; and, in fact, UNESCO's inscription on what makes washoku worth preserving sounds vague enough to apply to almost any culture's cuisine: 'special meals and beautifully decorated dishes using fresh ingredients… served on special tableware and shared by family members' made from 'various natural, locally sourced ingredients.' Sorry mate, but add 'with a great selection of craft beer' and that sounds like copy from a press release for a Shoreditch small plates joint. The only thing that really elevates Japanese gastronomy above any other country's is the efficacy of its marketing.

Not only is Japanese food not particularly unique in terms of its guiding principles, it's also just as connected to the world around it as anywhere else. Tempura comes from the Portuguese. Sushi comes from Southeast Asia (sort of). Noodles come from China. Actually, a LOT of stuff comes from China. So where's China's UNESCO listing?!

And then, of course, there's *yoshoku*. Yoshoku is Japanese 'Western' food, encompassing an array of dishes not seen as 'traditional' Japanese food, like *omurice* and okonomiyaki. Most yoshoku dishes wouldn't be recognisable as Western anywhere in the West, and although many of them have been a part of Japanese gastronomy for decades or even centuries, they still aren't considered quite Japanese. In fact, yoshoku is sort of a catch-all for non-washoku dishes generally; curry rice, for example, wouldn't be thought of as Western, but it's not Japanese either – so it is called yoshoku. However, Japanese food that originates from within the East Asian neighbourhood, like gyoza, ramen and mentaiko, fall into a kind of third, nameless category. One of the most popular and delicious of these culinary orphans is yakiniku: Japanese Korean barbecue.

Grilling meat over charcoal is a universal thing, of course, so in a way it's odd to attribute it to any one particular country anyway. So you could say that yakiniku is a Japanese thing, just like yakitori, but the cuts and condiments used are simply too indebted to Korean barbecue to say it's independently Japanese. In fact, it is often billed explicitly as Korean, especially in Shin-Okubo, the unofficial 'Koreatown' of Tokyo. Here, yakiniku restaurants number in the dozens, but really it's common all over town. After all, who can resist tender meat, marinated with salt and sugar and spice, then grilled over charcoal?

Like yakitori, there are too many varieties of yakiniku to provide recipes individually, so what follows are recipes for a couple of marinades and sauces and a general guide on what cuts will work, and how to cook them.

国
際
都
市
の
東
京

Where to find
Kurumu くるむ
Shin-Okubo, 〒169-0072, wowsokb.jp/curumu

YAKINIKU CAN INCLUDE JUST ABOUT
ANY CUT (SEE ALSO HORUMON-YAKI,
PAGE 127), BUT A FEW OF THE MORE
POPULAR ITEMS ARE:

KALBI

Beef short ribs, cut away from the bone in long, thin
sheets.

TAN

Beef tongue, often pre-cooked until tender and then
sliced before grilling.

HATSU

Beef heart, an exceptionally flavourful and lean cut
particularly well suited to the high heat and strong
marinades typical of yakiniku.

BUTABARA

Pork belly, thinly sliced like bacon.

P-TORO

The porcine equivalent of 'toro' in tuna is not a
particular cut, but simply a highly marbled, juicy bit
of pig; it can come from either the jowl, or the centre of
the collar – what is called 'presa' in Spanish butchery.

Yakiniku can be marinated before cooking, or simply
cooked as is and then dipped in a flavourful sauce (but
marinated cuts are also served with a complementary
dip, such as ponzu, creamy sesame sauce, or simply
raw beaten egg). Vegetables are an important part of
a yakiniku meal, providing value, bulk and nutrition (as
well as lovely flavours in and of themselves), including
Korean-style pickles like kimchi or seasoned bean
sprouts on the side, or cabbage, kabocha squash,
peppers and shiitake to grill. Bowls of rice complete
the meal, and it all gets washed down with plenty of
beer, soju, sake or *makgeolli* – a kind of cloudy,
cider-like fermented rice beverage with a tangy
Yakult-like flavour.

These can be used as dipping sauces or as marinades;
as sauces, they will serve 2; as marinades, it will be
enough for about 500 g (1 lb 2 oz) of meat.

YAKINIKU SAUCE

6 tablespoons soy sauce
1½ tablespoons caster (superfine) sugar
1½ tablespoons sake
½ green apple, peeled and finely grated
15–30 g (½–1 oz) piece of ginger root, peeled
    and finely grated
1 big garlic clove, finely grated
1½ teaspoons sesame oil
1½ teaspoons white sesame seeds, toasted until
    deep golden brown, then crushed

METHOD

Stir everything together until the sugar dissolves.
For best results, leave for at least an hour before
using for the ginger and garlic to infuse.

KIMCHI SAUCE

100 g (3½ oz) kimchi
1½ tablespoons caster (superfine) sugar
1½ tablespoons mirin
1 tablespoon gochujang
1 tablespoon vegetable oil
1 teaspoon sesame oil

METHOD

Blitz everything together in a blender or food
processor until reasonably smooth.

国
際
都
市
の
東
京

UNI LINGUINI

SEA URCHIN LINGUINI

The timeline of Tokyo history is one long noodle. Soba and udon have been enjoyed here for at least 400 years, and other forms of Tokyo noodlecraft date back to as early as the 8th century. But traditional Japanese noodles aren't the only ones you're likely to encounter in Tokyo. Far from it. In fact, Tokyoites' love for noodles is fairly indiscriminate, and you'll find varieties from all over the world here, including, of course, Italian pasta. Japan's love affair with pasta began around World War II, when a number of factors ushered the exotic dish into Japanese kitchens. European cuisine in general became fashionable around the 1920s, and by the 1940s, spaghetti appeared in many high-end Western restaurants around Tokyo and Yokohama. Just like Japanese curry, Japanese pasta mutated into something quite distinct from the original source material, often incorporating odd local flavours. Perhaps the most famous Japanese pasta dish is 'Spaghetti Napolitan', a preparation inspired by American military rations that features ketchup and frankfurters as two of its primary ingredients (don't tell me you haven't eaten something similar when you were a student).

As Japanese pasta has evolved over the decades, it's become very much its own thing, different from what you'd find in Italy but nonetheless extremely delicious. One of the most common flavourings for pasta in Japan is various types of seafood roe or other innards, such as the spicy cod roe called mentaiko, or dark crab meat. But the crème de la crème of Japanese sea creature gonad-based pasta dishes is uni pasta, made from ripe, briny sea urchin. The iodine-rich, concentrated shellfish flavour combines beautifully with supple pasta, and the flavour to me is both 100% Japanese and 100% Italian.

SERVES 4

150 g (5 oz) sea urchin roe (fresh or frozen)
50 g (2 oz) dark crab meat
juice of ¼ lemon
100 g (3½ oz) butter, melted
salt, to taste
400 g (14 oz) dried linguini
pinch of shichimi togarashi
20 g (¾ oz) Parmesan, grated
12 g (½ oz) chives, finely chopped
40 g (1½ oz) salmon roe
a few leaves fresh dill or basil, torn

151

METHOD

Whisk or blend together the sea urchin, crab meat and lemon juice. Whisk in the melted butter, a little at a time, as if you were making a mayonnaise or hollandaise. Season with salt, taste and adjust as necessary.

Cook the pasta in boiling salted water until al dente, then drain and return to the pan, reserving a little of the pasta water. Leave to cool for a minute or two – if you add the sauce when it's too hot, the emulsion will break. Stir in the sauce, adding a little bit of the pasta water to slacken the sauce, if needed. Divide among 4 bowls and top with a tiny bit of shichimi, then the Parmesan, chives, salmon roe and dill or basil.

国
際
都
市
の
東
京

MAPO RAMEN

SICHUAN-SPICED TOFU NOODLES

152

Japan and China have a long, complicated, frequently antagonistic relationship. While the atrocities committed by the Japanese during World War II have not been forgotten in China, and Japan does itself no favours by perpetually refusing to apologise or fully accept wrongdoing, Japanese culture is surprisingly fashionable in China. Anime and manga as well as sushi and matcha are very popular in cities like Shanghai and Beijing, which is a weird sort of reversal of the direction culture has generally flowed for the vast majority of history. So much of Japanese culture has direct, traceable roots in China: everything from religion and orthography to tea bowls and noodles. And despite the political issues between the two countries, there's still a lot of positive cultural exchange between them. One of the more interesting examples of this is ramen, a dish that in Japan many still consider Chinese, but that can now be found all over China, sold as a distinctly Japanese dish.

Even more complex is the recent trend of 'mapo ramen' in Tokyo: a combination of a traditional Chinese dish (mapo tofu) with a Japanese version of a Chinese dish (ramen), the result of which is very Chinese in terms of flavour, but that wouldn't be found in China. It's a kind of culinary orphan, neither Japanese nor Chinese but also kind of both. But then again, who cares? It's really delicious and that's all that matters.

SERVES 4

600–700 g (1 lb 5 oz–1 lb 9 oz/2 packs) firm or
    extra firm silken tofu
water
big pinch of salt
2 tablespoons Sichuan pepper
4 dried red Chinese chillies
4 tablespoons vegetable oil
2 anchovy fillets (optional)
1 bird's eye chilli (or more, to taste), finely sliced
4 garlic cloves, finely sliced
15 g (½ oz) piece of ginger root, peeled and
    finely shredded
300 g (10½ oz) minced (ground) pork
1 tablespoon preserved black beans
80 g (3 oz) doubanjiang
1½ tablespoons caster (superfine) sugar
500 ml (17 fl oz/2 cups) chicken stock
1 tablespoon sesame oil

1½ tablespoons cornflour (cornstarch), mixed to
    a paste with a little water
Worcestershire sauce and/or soy sauce, to taste
4 portions thick ramen noodles
small handful of coriander (cilantro), roughly torn
sesame seeds, toasted until deep golden brown
plenty of sansho pepper

METHOD

Cut the tofu into 2.5-cm (1-in) cubes and bring the water to a low simmer along with the salt. Carefully add the tofu to the salted water and poach for 10 minutes. Remove gently with a slotted spoon.

Toast the Sichuan pepper and dried chillies in a dry frying pan (skillet) until aromatic and beginning to colour, then leave to cool and grind to a coarse powder. Add the oil to the pan and place over a high heat, then add the anchovies, if using, and the bird's eye chilli. Fry for a minute or two, then add the garlic, ginger and pork and fry until the pork is browned. Add the black beans, doubanjiang, sugar and the ground Sichuan pepper and chillies. Cook for a few minutes, stirring often, so the flavours meld. Add the chicken stock and sesame oil and bring to the boil, then stir in some (not all) of the cornflour-water mixture. Let the sauce boil for a few minutes to thicken, stirring continuously; add more cornflour slurry if you want it thicker (it should be quite thick so it clings well to the noodles). Taste the sauce and adjust seasoning with Worcestershire and/or soy sauces. Gently stir in the tofu, using a pushing motion with the back of your spatula and shaking the pan to coat the tofu without breaking it up.

Bring a large pot of water to a rolling boil and cook the noodles until al dente. Drain well, then transfer to 4 bowls. Top with the hot tofu mixture and garnish with the coriander, sesame seeds and sansho.

国際都市の東京

┌───┐
Where to find

Akazukin あかずきん
Soshigaya-Okura, 〒157-0073,
soshigaya-minami.sakura.ne.jp
└───┘

EBIKATSU BURGER

BREADED PRAWN PATTY BURGER

My first trip to Tokyo was back in 2002, on a package holiday that my parents bought me as a high school graduation present. It was an amazing trip, of course, but even for someone who was already a keen Japanophile and very into Japanese food, it was a bit overwhelming at times.

That first night in Shinjuku was so disorientating I can't remember many details, but I do remember where we eventually went for dinner: a fast-food chain restaurant called First Kitchen, which I think we decided on because they had a picture menu with some English on it. I had taken a two-week Japanese language course so I knew some basics, but of course that was completely useless when confronted with the unforgiving reality of complicated text and native speech – and trying to order food even with the picture menu and a very accommodating and patient cashier to help us was extremely difficult. I wanted a number three set meal and just kept pointing to what I wanted and saying 'san' ('three') – what I didn't know is that Japanese numbers are given one of dozens of suffixes or modifiers to indicate their meaning. For example, 'number three' is *sanban*, three things is *mittsu*, three people is *sannin*, three cups is *sanbai*, three days is *mikka*, three small animals is *sanbiki*, and three guns or palanquins is *sanchō*. So just saying 'san' is basically nonsense. But somehow we got there in the end... only to then discover there were follow-up questions about seasoning and condiments (see Flavour Potato, page 158). Cue more confusion and futile gesticulation.

I think most people have a similar experience on their first visit to Japan – as hospitable as people are there, it is very tricky to figure things out without knowing the language. But even though it was stressful to order, the food was delicious in the end, and First Kitchen remained a favourite Japanese fast-food chain throughout my time living there. My go-to order was the ebikatsu burger – a breaded and deep-fried prawn patty on a soft bun with shredded cabbage, tonkatsu sauce and tartare sauce. Think Filet-O-Fish, but waaaaay better.

SERVES 4

For the katsu
50 g (2 oz) firm silken tofu
1 tablespoon mayonnaise
¼ small onion, grated
20 g (¾ oz) cornflour (cornstarch) or potato starch
100 g (3½ oz) cod, haddock or other white fish
pinch of salt and white pepper
250 g (9 oz) raw prawns (shrimp), shelled and deveined
40 g (1½ oz/⅓ cup) plain (all-purpose) flour
1 egg, beaten with a little water
50 g (2 oz/¾ cup) panko
oil, for shallow or deep frying

For the tartare sauce
40 g (1½ oz) gherkins, finely diced
10 g (½ oz) chives, finely sliced
juice of ¼ lemon
1 egg, hard-boiled, peeled and mashed
100 g (3½ oz) mayo
pinch of MSG
a few tarragon or parsley leaves, coarsely chopped
1 teaspoon Dijon mustard

To serve
oil, for shallow frying (at least 2 tablespoons)
4 burger buns
¼ hispi cabbage, finely shredded
4 tablespoons tonkatsu sauce

METHOD

To make the katsu, blend the tofu, mayo, onion, starch, fish, salt and pepper in a food processor until it forms a paste. Coarsely mince (grind) the prawns either with a knife or with the food processor (make sure you don't blend them too much – they should still have plenty of texture). Combine the prawns with the fish paste and divide into 4 portions. Oil your hands and shape each portion into a patty about 1.5 cm (⅝ in) thick. Freeze for at least an hour. Dredge the patties in the flour, then in the egg and then the panko. Refrigerate until needed.

For the tartare sauce, stir everything together until well combined. To serve, heat the oil in a frying pan (skillet) over a medium heat. Fry the ebikatsu on each side for about 4 minutes until golden. Drain on paper towels and construct the burgers: place a spoonful of tartare sauce on the bottom bun, then the cabbage, then the tonkatsu sauce, then the ebikatsu and then more tartare sauce.

154

国際都市の東京

FLAVOUR POTATO

SHAKE-AND-SEASON FRENCH FRIES

In 2016, First Kitchen was acquired by Wendy's, and over the past few years they have merged their restaurants together under the awkward name 'Wendy's First Kitchen'. Luckily, they have kept the best First Kitchen item on the new menu: their famous Flavour Potato, a fast-food innovation so ingenious, I really don't know why it hasn't caught on elsewhere. Basically, you are given your fries in a paper bag with a sachet of powdered flavouring on the side; you dump in the seasoning and shake the bag, coating each fry with a dust of intense, tangy flavour. The flavours themselves are brilliant – sometimes familiar (like roasted garlic), sometimes fancy (chicken consommé) and sometimes Japanese (shoyu butter). The following are a few of my favourites. The fries in the recipe are thin and they still have their skin on. You can really use any kind of fries or chips (or even roasted potatoes).

ENOUGH FOR ABOUT
4 PORTIONS OF FRIES

NORI BUTTER

1 tablespoon butter powder
1 tablespoon aonori
¼ teaspoon MSG
¼ teaspoon fine salt

CONSOMMÉ

1 tablespoon Chinese chicken stock powder
1 teaspoon beef stock powder
¼ teaspoon onion granules
¼ teaspoon shiitake or porcini mushroom powder
¼ teaspoon dried parsley
¼ teaspoon tomato powder (available online, optional)
pinch of salt
pinch of finely ground pepper

国
際
都
市
の
東
京

MENTAIKO

1 tablespoon bottarga, finely grated, or mentaiko/tarako-flavoured furikake (available at Japanese supermarkets), finely ground
2 teaspoons Korean chilli powder, finely ground
1 teaspoon dashi powder, finely ground
¼ teaspoon caster (superfine) sugar
¼ teaspoon salt

SERVES 4

800 g (1 lb 12 oz) floury potatoes, skins on, cut into 5-mm (¼-in) fries
2 litres (70 fl oz/8 cups) water
2 tablespoons white rice vinegar
2 tablespoons salt
vegetable oil, for deep-frying (groundnut (peanut) oil is good for these but any will do)

METHOD

Keep your cut potatoes submerged in a bowl of cold water until ready to use. Bring the water to the boil along with the vinegar and salt, then add the potatoes and boil for 10 minutes. Drain carefully so as to not break the potatoes too much, then spread them out on a baking sheet lined with paper towels. Leave to air-dry and cool slightly for 10 minutes.

Heat at least 1.5 litres (52 fl oz/6 cups) of oil to 200°C (400°F). If you don't have a thermometer, place a single chip in the hot oil as it is heating up. When it is sizzling rapidly and beginning to colour, you can add one-third of the fries and cook for 1 minute, stirring as they fry, then remove and drain on paper towel. Repeat with the remaining potatoes, allowing the oil to come back up to 200°C (400°F) in between batches. Leave the par-fried potatoes to cool completely, then transfer to the fridge, uncovered, until cold. Or, for best results, freeze them overnight before proceeding.

Reheat the oil to 200°C (400°F). Fry the fries in batches for about 3–4 minutes, until golden brown and crisp. Drain on paper towels. To serve, divide the fries into paper bags and serve with the seasonings on the side. Add about ½ tablespoon of the seasoning to each serving and shake the bag to coat the fries.

Where to find

Wendy's First Kitchen
ウェンディーズファーストキッチン
Multiple locations, wendys-firstkitchen.co.jp

Tokyo Global

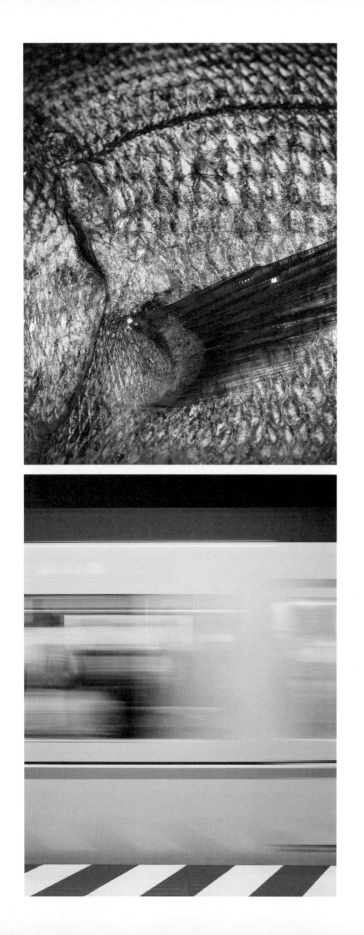

CRAB SHUMAI

STEAMED PORK AND CRAB OPEN WONTONS

162

Often, Chinese dishes become incorporated into Japanese gastronomy to the extent that they become their own Japanese thing, like ramen, gyoza, fried rice or nikuman. But other Chinese dishes retain their Chinese identity despite a long presence in Japan. One of these is *shumai*, steamed parcels of pork or seafood nested in a delicate wonton. While gyoza can be found at any ordinary ramen shop, izakaya or home kitchen in Tokyo, shumai, for some reason, are a bit more specialised. They're served at Chinese restaurants, of course, but perhaps most commonly seen in department store food halls, steamed en masse in enormous bamboo baskets. Like most dumplings, shumai are always delightful, so it's nice to know that in Tokyo you're never very far from somewhere that can satisfy your steamed seafood cravings.

MAKES ABOUT 30 SHUMAI (BUT THIS WILL DEPEND ON THE SIZE OF YOUR WONTONS)

400 g (14 oz) minced (ground) pork
200 g (7 oz) crab meat (use a mix of 50/50 white and brown meat if you can)
1 tablespoon sesame oil
1 egg
½ onion, finely chopped
2 spring onions (scallions) or nira, finely sliced
½ teaspoon salt
¼ teaspoon ground white pepper
20–30 wonton wrappers
a little oil
50 g (2 oz) crab roe or orange fish roe (such as ikura or tobiko)
soy sauce or ponzu, to serve
chilli oil or hot mustard, to serve (optional)

METHOD

国際都市の東京

Combine the pork, crab, sesame oil, egg, onion, spring onions or nira, salt and pepper in a bowl and mix well. Place a heaped tablespoon of this mixture into the centre of each wonton, then gather up the sides around the mixture to form little parcels (the top should be left open). Line a steamer basket with baking parchment and coat it with a thin layer of oil using paper towel. Place the shumai in the basket and steam over boiling water for 10 minutes. Remove the basket and garnish each shumai with a little bit of roe, and serve with soy sauce or ponzu with chilli oil or mustard on the side for dipping.

Where to find
Shodoten 小洞天
Nihombashi, 〒103-0027, shodoten.com

POKE

HAWAIIAN RAW FISH SALAD

Poke is Hawaiian, but it would be easy to mistake it for a Japanese dish; it has many similarities to several traditional Japanese dishes and it originated among Hawaii's fishermen, many of whom were of Japanese descent. But weirdly, it's not the Hawaiian speciality that's really taken Tokyo by storm – that would be the Hawaiian pancake. Hawaiian pancake shops have sprung up all over Tokyo in the past decade or so, serving thick, super-fluffy pancakes often garnished with piles of fruit and whipped cream. The problem is, I can find zero evidence that they're actually Hawaiian; really, this style of pancake is just American – Japanese pancakes, or 'hotcakes', are smaller and denser in comparison. But Hawaii is a powerful brand in Japan – it's a perpetually popular destination for Japanese holidaymakers due to proximity, cultural affinities, sometimes familial connections and, of course, all the other reasons that everybody loves Hawaii, like the weather and beaches and coffee and the fact that Obama is from there. So it's actually pretty easy to find good Hawaiian food in Tokyo – just look beyond the pancakes and you'll find dozens of restaurants serving kalua pork, loco moco and, of course, poke.

Poke is endlessly customisable, by the way; this is a basic recipe but you can embellish it however you like (with some suggestions opposite).

SERVES 4

2 heaped tablespoons wakame or similar seaweed
zest and juice of 1 lime
1 small red chilli, thinly sliced
4 tablespoons soy sauce
2 tablespoons sesame oil
1 tablespoon caster (superfine) sugar
½ tablespoon rice vinegar
(500–600 g/1 lb 2 oz–1 lb 5 oz) very fresh raw tuna, salmon, hamachi, swordfish or similar meaty fish (boneless and skinless) or you can use cooked octopus
1 small sweet onion, diced (if you can get Maui or Vidalia or Cipollini, they are the best)
1 ripe avocado
½ cucumber
100 g (3½ oz) cherry tomatoes, halved
50 g (2 oz) samphire or similar fresh seaweed (optional)
40 g (1½ oz) macadamia nuts, roasted until golden brown, then coarsely chopped
½ tablespoon white sesame seeds, toasted until deep golden brown
2 spring onions (scallions), finely sliced

For the embellishments
crispy fried onions, furikake of your choosing, shiso leaves, fish roe, chilli flakes or shichimi, diced tropical fruit, etc.

165

METHOD

Rehydrate the wakame in warm water for about 30 minutes. Stir together the lime, chilli, soy sauce, sesame oil, sugar and rice vinegar. Cut the fish or octopus into 2.5-cm (1-in) cubes and cut the avocado and cucumber into 1-cm (½-in) cubes. Break the samphire into bite-size pieces, discarding any woody bits. Mix together the fish, vegetables, seaweeds and dressing.

This can be eaten immediately, but it is better if you have time to leave it to marinate for at least an hour. It can be eaten with rice, or simply on its own. Garnish with the macadamia nuts, sesame, spring onions and anything else you like.

国際都市の東京

Where to find
Popopeku ポポペク
Hatsudai, 〒151-0071, popopeku.jp

NAIR-STYLE CURRY RICE

166

The arrival of curry in Japan is delightfully circuitous. Japan has always been the terminus of various cultural pathways that snake their way through Asia (Buddhism is a particularly notable example), so you'd think that curry would have come to Japan directly from countries with a curry tradition, like India or Malaysia, perhaps via China. But no. Japanese curry is actually based on British versions of Indian curry, which were introduced in the late 19th century. These curries were – and typically still are – classified as Western food, and indeed the way they are cooked is more similar to a British or French stew, thickened with roux as opposed to the mixtures of molten onions, tomatoes, ghee, yoghurt, coconut milk, nuts, etc. that you'd find in real subcontinental curries. The result is a curry that's more like a lightly spiced gravy, and while it doesn't have much in common with the curries of India, it has a certain charm nonetheless. A few historical recipes for this type of curry have surfaced on the internet recently and, amazingly, they aren't very different at all from modern Japanese curry rice.

Of course, you can also get 'real' Indian curries in Tokyo, but even these often take the familiar format of a Japanese curry, with pieces of meat and vegetables swimming in a wide lake of sauce, served on a plate with a mound of Japanese rice off to one side. At Nair's, the oldest Indian curry house in Japan, you can get a taste of this slightly Japanised but still mainly Indian curry in the form of their enduring Murugi Lunch, apparently unchanged since the restaurant opened in 1949. The curry itself is based on an old Keralan recipe, but it's plated Japanese-style with a dome of rice (Japanese rice, no less, but flavoured with turmeric) on the side, and also, unusually, a bit of mashed potato and boiled cabbage. The chicken is braised in the sauce for 7 hours until it effortlessly slips off the bone, and the dish is eaten by mixing everything together. It's an idiosyncratic but delicious dish, and it's a rare chance to taste a bit of living curry history.

SERVES 2, BUT THE PORTION IS LARGE SO YOU MAY BE ABLE TO STRETCH IT TO 4

For the curry
4 tablespoons vegetable oil
2 onions, finely chopped
2 garlic cloves, grated
15 g (½ oz) piece of ginger root, peeled and grated
2 tablespoons Japanese or Madras curry powder
½ tablespoon garam masala
1 teaspoon ground cumin
400 g (14 oz/large) tin of peeled plum tomatoes, puréed, or passata (sieved tomatoes)
2 teaspoons caster (superfine) sugar
1 teaspoon salt
2 whole chicken legs, bone-in and skin on
250 ml (8½ fl oz/1 cup) chicken stock

For the rice
300 g (10½ oz/1½ cups) rice
1 teaspoon turmeric
15 g (½ oz) butter

For the potatoes
2 baking potatoes, peeled and cut into chunks
pinch of salt
¼ teaspoon cumin
¼ teaspoon ground coriander
pinch of turmeric
2 tablespoons peas, blanched
¼ hispi or flat cabbage, roughly chopped

国
際
都
市
の
東
京

METHOD

Heat the oil in a deep flameproof, ovenproof casserole over a medium heat, then add the onions. Fry the onions for 10–15 minutes with the lid on, stirring frequently, so they steam as they fry, until the onions are golden brown. Add the garlic and ginger and continue to cook for about 5 minutes. Add the spices and reduce the heat to medium-low, and stir the spices to infuse them into the oil and onion mixture. Add the tomatoes, sugar and salt and stir to combine, then lower in the chicken legs. Add the chicken stock and just enough water to cover the chicken, if necessary. Reduce the heat to very very low, place a lid on the pan and cook for 7 hours (or less, it's kind of up to you). You can also do this in an oven set to 120°C (250°F/gas ¼). Check the curry every hour or so to make sure the liquid hasn't reduced too much – the chicken should be covered at all times, so top up with water as needed.

When the curry is just about ready to serve, cook the rice according to the instructions on page 26, but add the turmeric and butter to the pan before cooking. Boil the potatoes until soft, then coarsely mash together with the salt, spices and peas.

Just before serving, boil the cabbage for a couple of minutes, until tender. To serve, scoop the rice into small bowls and unmould onto wide plates to form little domes. Place the chicken on the side of the rice and cover with the sauce. Serve the mashed potatoes and cabbage on top. Mix everything together before tucking in.

国際都市の東京

CRISPY PATA

Filipinos are Japan's third-largest non-Japanese demographic, with a population of around 300,000, compared to 500,000 Koreans and 700,000 Chinese. But while those communities are a visible, often prominent part of Tokyo's culinary landscape, Filipino food (and culture, generally) is seldom seen. There are many reasons for this, including a lack of familiarity with Filipino cuisine among the Japanese, and the fact that many Filipinos in Japan save their spare earnings to send back to family in the Philippines, rather than spending it on restaurants – the Central Bank of the Philippines has reported that Filipino workers in Japan remit in excess of one billion USD back to the Philippines each year. But even though you might not just happen upon Filipino food in Tokyo the way you definitely would with Korean or Chinese food, that doesn't mean it isn't there. There are several Filipino bars and restaurants serving classics like *menudo*, *kare-kare*, and *sisig* scattered around the city, but you do have to look to find them. One in particular worth seeking out is New Nanay's, located centrally in Roppongi. Regulars especially love Nanay's lunchtime buffets, an incredibly good-value option to try a number of Filipino dishes in one go, but the à la carte options are where you'll find the really good stuff. The crispy pata – twice-cooked pork leg – comes highly recommended.

Traditionally, this recipe calls for a cut of pork that is very large and difficult to find – essentially the lower half of the leg from the knee down, so the hock and the trotter as one unbroken cut. But you can use pretty much any joint of pork with the skin on to make this – the method will be basically the same.

SERVES 4-6

1 kg (2 lb 4 oz) skin-on boneless pork joint such as leg or shoulder, or 1.5 kg (3 lb 5 oz) skin-on, bone-in pork joint such as hocks or ham
6 bay leaves
2 tablespoons whole black peppercorns
1½ teaspoons salt
3–4 litres (105–140 fl oz/12–16 cups) water (enough to cover the knuckles)
150 ml (5 fl oz/scant ⅔ cup) vinegar
50 ml (1¾ fl oz/3 tablespoons) soy sauce
2 tablespoons soft brown sugar
½ onion, finely diced
1–2 bird's eye chillies, finely sliced
oil, as needed
salt and pepper and garlic powder, to taste

METHOD

Place the pork in a large saucepan with the bay, peppercorns, salt and enough water to cover. Bring to a simmer and cook until the pork is tender, about 1 hour.

Meanwhile, combine the vinegar, soy sauce, brown sugar, onion and chillies in a pan over a low heat and stir to dissolve the sugar. Remove the pork from the cooking liquor and leave to cool and air-dry.

Preheat the oven to 280ºC (500ºF/maximum gas). Rub the cooked pork with the oil, salt, pepper and garlic powder, then place in a baking pan and transfer to the oven. Cook for another hour until the skin is bronze and crispy. (Traditionally this is deep-fried to crisp the skin, but because the pork joints are so big, I would not recommend trying this at home.) Leave to cool slightly before removing the meat from the bone and cutting into large chunks. Serve with the vinegar sauce on the side for dipping.

国
際
都
市
の
東
京

Where to find
New Nanay's ニューナナイズ Roppongi, 〒106-0032

CHOUX CREAM

CRUNCHY PROFITEROLES WITH VANILLA CREAM

170

French pastries are perhaps even more ubiquitous in Tokyo than traditional Japanese sweets. Any department store basement will have a large section devoted to them, and many train stations have a pâtissière as well, inevitably competing with the conbini for on-the-go snack sales. And then there are the countless independent bakeries selling all manner of delightful cakes, Viennoiserie and enriched breads. But perhaps the most popular pastry in Tokyo is the simple choux cream, or cream puff: a tennis ball-sized hollow of choux pastry, filled with a light and cool vanilla cream, often topped with a layer of crunchy 'craquelin' cookie crust.

MAKES 8 PUFFS

For the crème pâtissière

3 egg yolks
45 g (1¾ oz/scant ¼ cup) caster (superfine) sugar
25 g (1 oz/scant ¼ cup) sponge flour or plain (all-purpose) flour, sifted
1 vanilla pod, split and seeds scraped
250 ml (8½ fl oz/1 cup) milk
200 ml (7 fl oz/scant 1 cup) whipping cream

For the craquelin

85 g (3¼ oz) cold butter
100 g (3½ oz/scant ½ cup) caster (superfine) sugar
100 g (3½ oz/heaped ¾ cup) sponge flour or plain (all-purpose) flour, plus extra for dusting

For the choux pastry

50 g (2 oz) butter
pinch of salt
120 ml (4 fl oz/½ cup) water
75 g (2½ oz/scant ⅔ cup) sponge flour or plain (all-purpose) flour
2 eggs

METHOD

To make the crème pâtissière, whisk together the egg yolks and sugar until the sugar dissolves, then mix in the flour and whisk until smooth. Place the vanilla seeds and pod in a saucepan with the milk and bring to a simmer. Remove from the heat and gradually stir into the egg yolk mixture and mix until smooth. Return to the pan and bring to a simmer, stirring constantly, and cook until the mixture thickens to a batter consistency. Cover and transfer to the fridge to chill completely.

Whip the cream to soft peaks, then fold in the cooled crème pâtissière and mix until completely smooth. Transfer to a piping bag fitted with a wide metal nozzle and refrigerate until needed.

For the craquelin, mash the butter and sugar with a fork until it forms a pebbly texture, then add the flour and mix with the fork until to make a loose crumb. Dust your work surface with a little flour and tip the crumb onto it, then work it lightly with your hands to a smooth dough the consistency of modelling clay. Wrap in cling film (plastic wrap) and rest it in the fridge for 1 hour.

Unwrap the dough and roll it out to a thickness of 3 mm (⅛ in) between 2 sheets of cling film or baking parchment. Return to the fridge and chill completely. Cut out rounds of dough using a 3-cm (½-in) cutter, then freeze them in a single layer on a tray or plate.

To make the choux pastry, melt the butter in a saucepan and add the salt and water. Bring to a simmer, then remove from the heat, add the flour and whisk to combine. Place the pan back on the heat and beat the mixture with a spatula until it dries out slightly and reaches a consistency like mashed potato. Remove from the heat and tip the dough into a bowl. Leave to cool for a few minutes, then mix in the eggs with a spatula, one at a time, until fully incorporated into the dough. Transfer to a piping bag, and cut the tip of the bag to an opening of about 2 cm (¾ in).

Preheat the oven to 180°C (350°F/gas 4). Line a baking sheet with baking parchment and pipe the choux pastry straight down into little blobs about 4 cm (1½ in) in diameter. Top each blob with a round of frozen craquelin dough, then bake for 25 minutes until fully inflated and a rich golden brown. Remove from the oven and leave to cool completely. Jab the pastry cream bag tip into the bottom of each puff and fill with the cream. Refrigerate until needed, but these are best consumed within a couple of hours.

国際都市の東京

TOTORO CHOUX CREAM

The biggest name in choux cream in Tokyo is probably the chain Beard Papa, which I have to say is not worth visiting at all – I can't tell you how disappointing it is, especially in a city that's absolutely silly for cream puffs. Instead, head to Shirohige's Cream Puff Factory in Western Tokyo, not far from Shimokitazawa, an area known for its funky second-hand shops and hip restaurants. Shirohige may not make the best choux cream in Tokyo, but he definitely makes the cutest, baked in the shape of Totoro, the *kawaii* forest creature of the Studio Ghibli classic, My Neighbour Totoro. (Shirohige, by the way, means 'white beard' – possibly a little dig at Beard Papa, or possibly a reference to director Hayao Miyazaki's famous white mane.) But if you can't make it there, you can actually recreate the experience at home – and actually, it's surprisingly easy to make shapes out of choux pastry, so get creative and try to replicate all your favourite Ghibli characters! (If you can make a convincing Howl's Moving Castle I'll be well impressed).

MAKES 8 PUFFS

Follow the instructions for the choux cream on page 170, but omit the craquelin and, this time, transfer the choux pastry to two piping bags; put about one-tenth of the mixture in one bag fitted with a 2-mm (⅛-in) metal nozzle and put the remainder in a separate one, cut open about 2 cm (¾ in) wide.

For the decoration
50 g (2 oz) ready-rolled white fondant
50 g (2 oz) ready-rolled brown fondant (optional)
100 g (3½ oz) milk chocolate, melted

METHOD

Preheat the oven to 180°C (350°F/gas 4). Line a tray with baking parchment and pipe the choux pastry from the wide-mouthed bag straight down into little blobs about 4 cm (1½ in) in diameter. Top each blob with two tiny 'ears' from the narrow-mouthed piping bag. Bake for 25 minutes until fully inflated and a rich golden brown. Remove from the oven and leave to cool completely, then fill with crème pâtissière as in the following recipe.

To decorate, cut out 16 little circles of the white fondant with a small, sharp knife to make the eyes. Spoon the melted chocolate into a disposable piping bag and snip of the end. Then, pipe a blob onto the fondant circles to create the pupils. Make the nose by either cutting them out of the brown fondant or by piping the melted chocolate onto the choux creams.

国
際
都
市
の
東
京

Where to find

Shirohige's 白髭のシュークリーム工房
Setagaya-Daita, 〒155-0033, shiro-hige.com

'TOO MANY TOURISTS!'
SAID I, AS I WALKED AROUND
SENSŌ-JI TEMPLE

I SWIFTLY RETURNED
TO NAKAMISE-DORI
FOR AUTHENTIC CRAFTS:

SAMURAI T-SHIRT
AND A HELLO KITTY MASK

NEAPOLITAN PIZZA

176

Tokyo is pizza country. Though it might not appear to be the case at first glance, Tokyoites have embraced pizza in much the same way New Yorkers have, devouring everything from the finest authentic Italian-style pie all the way down to the cheapest, dirtiest slice. Pizza in Tokyo ranges from Domino's-esque mass-produced delivery stuff up to some of the most carefully crafted 'za you'll ever encounter, and the world (including, sometimes grudgingly, the Italians) have taken notice. This is because Tokyo pizzaiolos haven't just perfected their craft; they've taken it a step further, imbuing it with a distinctly Japanese ethos, flavour and identity. For example, at Pizza Studio Tamaki in Higashi-Azabu, chef Tsubasa Tamaki uses Japanese cedar chips to infuse his pizzas with a delicate but evocative whiff of peppery smoke. At Serinkan in Kamimeguro, chef Susumu Kakinuma has pioneered pizzacraft using only Japanese ingredients. And at Savoy in Azabu Juban, they've gone full fusion and put tuna sashimi, mayo and sweetcorn on a pizza.

That may sound like a step too far but, actually, completely bonkers things like that are among the most popular pizzas in Japan. If you have a look at the menu for Pizza La, one of the biggest pizza chains, you'll find all sorts of toppings that would probably make most Neapolitan pizzaiolos spit with disgust: mochi, Korean barbecue, teriyaki chicken, mayonnaise and potatoes, to name a few. And really, there's nothing wrong with that at all, especially if you put them on a proper light-yet-chewy, slightly charred Neapolitan pizza base. Therefore, this recipe is not for a traditional Neopolitan pizza, but features the Japanese twist of shellfish.

For the dough
800 g (1 lb 12 oz/6½ cups) '00' flour, plus extra for dusting
2 g fresh yeast
450 ml (15¾ fl oz/scant 2 cups) water
20 g (¾ oz) salt

For the toppings
400 g (14 oz) tin of tomatoes
300 g (10½ oz) fior de latte, cut into small pieces
100 g (3½ oz) squid, cut into bite-size pieces
100 g (3½ oz) raw prawns (shrimp), peeled and deveined
100 g (3½ oz) crab meat (white or 50/50 white and dark)
zest of ½ lemon
red chilli flakes (optional)
16–20 basil leaves
good olive oil

METHOD

To make the dough, place the flour in a deep bowl and form a well in the centre. Dissolve the yeast in the water, then pour into the well. Begin to mix the dough by pushing the flour into the liquid. When it starts to thicken, add the salt and continue to mix until it comes together. Tip the dough out onto a lightly floured surface and knead for 10–15 minutes. Leave to rest for 10 minutes, then knead it a few more times. Shape the dough into a ball, then divide into 4 equal portions. Roll these into balls and place onto a large tray, cover with cling film (plastic wrap) and leave to prove overnight.

Blitz the tomatoes in a blender until puréed but not too smooth. Roll or spread out the dough balls to about 25 cm (10 in) in diameter. Heat a non-stick, ovenproof frying pan (skillet) over a medium-high heat and preheat the grill to high. Lay the pizza bases, one at time, in the hot pan and cook for about 1 minute; while it's cooking, spread the tomato purée on top, leaving about 2.5 cm (1 in) uncovered along the outside, then scatter the cheese, squid, prawns and crab around the top. Transfer to the top rack of the oven and grill for another 2–3 minutes until the cheese has melted and the crust has cooked through and begun to blacken in spots. Garnish with a little freshly grated lemon zest, chilli flakes, basil leaves and a drizzle of olive oil.

国
際
都
市
の
東
京

Where to find

Pizza Studio Tamaki
Akabanebashi, 〒106-0044, pst-tk2-ad.com

AT HOME

4

KAMABOKO かまぼこ

YOKOZUNA 横綱

TERU TERU BOZU てるてる坊主

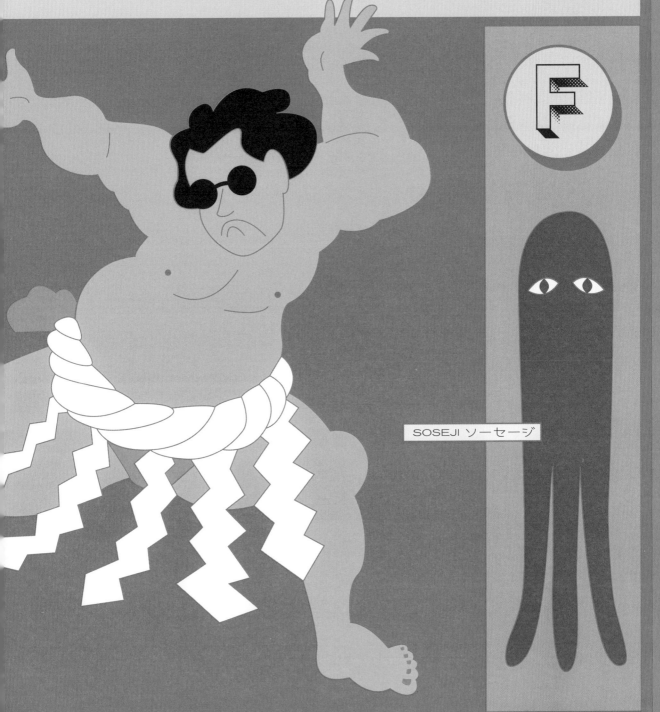

IN TOKYO

SOSEJI ソーセージ

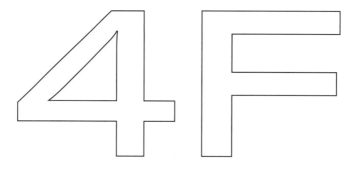

AT HOME IN TOKYO

A
T

H
O
M
E

I
N

T
O
K
Y
O

SMALL-SPACE, SIMPLE COOKING

There are so many great options for eating out in Tokyo that many flats are built with only the most rudimentary of kitchens - or some, no kitchen at all - and even though the city is crammed with great food, ordinary supermarkets where you might do a normal weekly shop are kind of hard to come by. That doesn't mean that Tokyoites don't cook - they just do so simply and creatively. A kitchen outfitted with only a two-ring electric burner, a rice cooker and a microwave or toaster oven may not sound like the best set-up to make great food, but so many Japanese dishes are inherently simple; and if you live in a tiny Tokyo apartment, that simplicity will become your best friend. These are the kind of cheap-and-cheerful, quick and easy meals you might prepare in a little flat, in Tokyo or wherever else you happen to be!

DASHI

FUNDAMENTAL JAPANESE BROTH

184

Dashi is the backbone of Japanese cookery, and while most Tokyoites will reach for the pre-packaged stuff or dashi powder the vast majority of the time (a shortcut I fully endorse), it's always good to know how to make dashi from scratch, as the flavour is exquisite and the ingredients are still useful even after they're cooked (see Onigiri, page 46 and Tsukudani, page 109). It's also really simple, and if you follow the steps for 'ichiban' and 'niban' (number one and number two) dashi, you can attain a large quantity of delicious homemade dashi for not very much money.

MAKES 500 ML (17 FL OZ/2 CUPS)
OF EACH DASHI, FOR A TOTAL OF
1 LITRE (34 FL OZ/4 CUPS) DASHI

ICHIBAN (NUMBER ONE) DASHI

10 g (½ oz) kombu (about a 10-cm (4-in) square), rinsed
600 ml (20 fl oz/2½ cups) water (it is best to use soft water like Volvic or Smart Water – it will provide a fuller flavour)
20 g (¾ oz) katsuobushi

Put the kombu in a saucepan and pour in the water. Place the pan on a low flame – kombu releases its flavour most readily at a temperature range from cold to just below the boiling point, so the more time you keep it in that range, the more flavourful your dashi will be. When the water barely begins to simmer, with just a few small bubbles breaking the surface of the water, add the katsuobushi, remove from the heat, and leave to infuse for about 15 minutes. Pass through a fine sieve and squeeze out the katsuobushi for maximum flavour.

NIBAN (NUMBER TWO) DASHI

600 ml (20 fl oz/2½ cups) water
used kombu and katsuobushi from making Ichiban Dashi (see opposite)

Niban dashi is not as delicious as ichiban dashi, but it is still great for most dishes where dashi is only required as a background flavour – so, for example, it's best to use it in something like *sukiyaki*, where sugar and soy sauce dominate, rather than in a bowl of udon, where the dashi is front and centre.

To make niban dashi, place the used kombu and katsuobushi in a saucepan with the fresh water and bring to the boil. Boil for about 10 minutes, then reduce to a very low simmer and cook for an additional 20 minutes. Turn off the heat and leave to infuse for 10–15 minutes, then pass through a fine sieve.

Or you can just use the powdered stuff, it's delicious and easy and cheap and everybody does it.

東京の家庭料理

JAPANESE BREAKFAST

Every time I go to Japan, I come back dedicated to eat a Japanese breakfast every day. The resolution never lasts, but that's not because it's difficult. It's because I'm a bit like a rat or other scavenger when it comes to breakfast – purely opportunistic, happy to eat whatever is available (hellooo, cold Domino's) but also happy to not eat anything at all. A traditional Japanese breakfast, like Japanese lunch or dinner, is a delightful multi-dish feast, and so easy to enjoy when it's laid out for you at a hotel or *ryokan* (traditional inn), but somewhat daunting if you have to make it yourself. But it's very easy with a little advance planning – just have the different elements on hand, prepared at the beginning of the week, and soon you'll be chowing down on a full Japanese every day.

MAKES ENOUGH FOR 5 BREAKFASTS

5 tablespoons miso
1½ teaspoons dashi powder
2 teaspoons white sesame seeds
1 spring onion (scallion), finely sliced
15 g (½ oz) wakame
300–350 g (10½–12 oz/1 block) silken tofu
250 g (9 oz/1¼ cups) rice
3 salmon fillets, cut into 5 equal portions
salt
5 eggs
5 portions natto (optional)
1 sheet of nori, cut into 10 strips
Japanese pickles

METHOD

First, make your own instant miso soup: mix together the miso, dashi powder, sesame seeds, spring onion and wakame. Cut the tofu into 1-cm (½-in) cubes. Keep the miso mixture and the tofu in the fridge in separate containers.

Cook the rice according to the instructions on page 27, then cool. Divide into 5 equal portions, wrap tightly in cling film (plastic wrap) and refrigerate.

Season the salmon liberally with salt and leave to absorb the seasoning for at least 1 hour – overnight is better. Grill on high heat until cooked through.

Cook the eggs *hanjuku* or *onsen* style. Hanjuku is sort of halfway between soft and hard boiled, mainly gooey in the middle but with a bit of set yolk. My method for perfect hanjuku eggs, using medium eggs, is to bring a pan of water to a rolling boil, then carefully lower in the eggs, and set a timer for 6½ minutes (for large eggs, cook them for 6 minutes and 50 seconds). When the timer is up, remove the eggs and transfer them to a cold water bath to stop the cooking. Keep in the fridge until needed.

For onsen eggs, use a water bath or immersion circulator to bring the water to 64°C (147°F) (you can also use a carefully watched saucepan and a thermometer for this). Cook the eggs for 1 hour, then remove and chill.

To serve, reheat the rice in the microwave. Place into bowls and top with the natto, if using. Place a spoonful of the miso soup mix into a bowl and add 150 ml (5 fl oz/scant ⅔ cup) of boiling water, whisk, and then add the tofu. Serve the egg, salmon, nori and pickles separately.

東
京
の
家
庭
料
理

BASIC BENTO

188

What would you pack in an ordinary lunchbox? A sandwich, no doubt. An apple or a banana, maybe some grapes. Carrot sticks? A packet of crisps? Granola bar? Ah, come on, let's go all out and throw some Oreos in there! You only live once.

There's nothing wrong with this sort of standard lunchbox. But it doesn't feel like a proper meal – you wouldn't really want to eat this stuff for dinner. In Japan, however, BENTO reign supreme. Bento are lunchboxes, but they don't compromise on the flavour, variety and presentation you'd expect from a full Japanese dinner – they're just miniaturised, neatly packed versions of the same kind of food: fish, meat, veg, rice. This makes them so much more satisfying than most lunches, and something to look forward to.

Because bento can contain pretty much anything you'd have for dinner, their varieties are infinite. Many are unique to a certain place – if you travel outside Tokyo, try to find an *ekiben* (train station bento) from wherever you go, even if you're just passing through. These contain local specialities and are a fantastic way to try new regional dishes. Then there are special holiday bento, some of the most impressive appearing at New Year's celebrations, packed with all sorts of exquisite delicacies like poached tiger prawns, pickled herring roe, braised chicken and root vegetables, and candied black beans and chestnuts. But even a basic bento is a lovely thing – with a variety of colour and flavour unrivalled by even the most ornate sandwich. This recipe is for just such a basic bento, and if it had a name it would be *makunouchi*, which means 'between acts' – they were originally packed as a light meal to be enjoyed during intermissions of lengthy *noh* or *kabuki* plays.

MAKES 5 BENTO (ENOUGH FOR A WORKING WEEK)

300 g (10½ oz/1½ cups) rice
500 ml (17 fl oz/2 cups) dashi
2 tablespoons soy sauce
1 tablespoon mirin
1 tablespoon caster (superfine) sugar
¼ teaspoon salt
10 tenderstem broccoli, cut into 2.5-cm (1-in) chunks
1 carrot, peeled and cut into 1-cm (½-in) thick rounds
120 g (4 oz) shelled edamame beans
8 eggs
1 tablespoon oil
6 frankfurters
5 umeboshi
100 g (3½ oz) Carrot and Daikon Namasu (page 198) or Japanese pickles such as takuan or asazuke
2 salmon fillets, cooked according to the instructions on page 187, and divided into 5 portions
a few pinches of black and white sesame seeds

METHOD

Cook the rice according to the instructions on page 27. Divide into 5 equal portions, wrap tightly in cling film (plastic wrap) and refrigerate.

Bring the dashi, soy sauce, mirin, sugar and salt to a high simmer. Cook the broccoli, carrot and edamame in the liquid until just tender, about 5 minutes. Remove with a slotted spoon and chill. Reserve the liquid.

Beat the eggs with 80 ml (3 fl oz/⅓ cup) of the dashi. Heat the oil over a medium-high heat in a small non-stick pan. Ladle some egg mixture into the pan – enough to cover the surface, like a thin crêpe. Cook until barely set, then use a small spatula to roll the egg up away from you, like a many-layered omelette. Add another spoonful of egg to the pan, and this time roll the egg up towards you. Repeat until all the egg mix is used up, then chill. Slice into 10 equal pieces.

Cut the franks in half, then form into octopuses by cutting them into 8 wedges, stopping halfway down their length, so they have a 'head' and 8 little 'arms'. Boil or grill the franks until their arms splay out.

Place the rice on one side of the box and top with an umeboshi in the centre. Arrange the pickles, salmon, egg and simmered veg on the other side of the box. Garnish the rice with black sesame and the veg with white sesame.

東
京
の
家
庭
料
理

OMURICE

SEASONED RICE TOPPED WITH AN OMELETTE

Omurice combines three of my all-time favourite comfort foods into one wonderful dish: eggs, fried rice and ketchup. It's so simple yet so satisfying, a perfect package of protein, fat and carbs, so cheap and easy to make, and yet so beautiful I'm actually getting a bit teary-eyed just thinking about it. Omurice is a dish that says 'I want you to feel full and content, I want you to get plenty of calories so you grow big and strong, and I want to put a smile on your face, because I love you.' There are restaurants in Tokyo (and probably home cooks) who have applied cheffy techniques to refine omurice, cooking the omelette just so and serving it with demiglace and that sort of thing. But really omurice doesn't need careful cooking or fine-dining embellishments to make it delicious; in fact, to me that's really the whole point of omurice. Just about anybody can make it, and it will always be delicious even at its most basic.

MAKES 1 BIG OMURICE
ENOUGH FOR 1 HUNGRY PERSON,
OR 2 NOT-THAT HUNGRY PERSONS
OR 2 HUNGRY PERSONS WHO ARE ALSO
EATING OTHER THINGS LIKE MISO SOUP
AND SALAD AND WHATNOT

30 g (1 oz) butter
1 banana shallot or small onion, diced
60 g (2 oz) shiitake mushrooms, destemmed and
    diced
1 chicken thigh, boneless and skinless, cut into 1-cm
    (½-in) cubes (optional)
300 g (10½ oz/1⅔ cups) cooked rice (from 150 g
    (5 oz/¾ cup) uncooked; rice that has been chilled
    in the fridge works best)
ketchup, to taste, plus extra to serve
soy sauce, to taste
salt and pepper, to taste
3 eggs, beaten with 1 tablespoon double
    (heavy) cream (optional)

METHOD

Melt half of the butter in a frying pan (skillet) over a medium heat, then sauté the shallot or onion until translucent. Add the shiitake and the chicken (if using) and sauté until the mushrooms soften and the chicken is cooked through. Add the rice, breaking up any clumps, and stir in the ketchup, soy sauce, salt and pepper.

Meanwhile, melt the remaining butter in a non-stick frying pan (skillet) over a medium-high heat, then tip in the beaten eggs and season with a little salt. Cook the egg until set on the bottom but still runny on top, then gently fold the eggs over themselves so the runny bit is now in the middle. Scoop the fried rice into a mound on a plate, then tip the omelette onto the top of the rice. Serve with more ketchup, if you like.

東
京
の
家
庭
料
理

SPINACH GOMA-AE

SPINACH WITH CRUSHED SESAME

TARAKO SPAGHETTI

COD'S ROE SPAGHETTI

Spinach *goma-ae* has got to be in the top 5 Japanese side dishes of all time, and it's easy to see why: it's easy, it's cheap, it's delicious, and it's healthy! Honestly, why are people so obsessed with things like ramen and sushi?! There should be a spinach goma-ae shop with a Michelin star.

194

This makes a lot of goma-ae so you can halve the recipe if you like. This stuff keeps well in the fridge for a few days and works well in a bento, so it's nice to have some on hand.

The Italians often use grated bottarga, or dried mullet roe, to add a strong yet subtle fishy flavour and massive umami boost to pasta dishes. The Japanese kind-of equivalent is pasta sauce made out of tarako, or cod's roe. Tarako spaghetti sauce is commonly sold in little sachets that you simply toss through hot pasta to make a quick and delicious meal, but it's easy to make yourself as well. If you like, you can use mentaiko, the spicy cured version of tarako, for a Korean chilli kick.

MAKES 8 LITTLE SIDE DISHES

4 tablespoons white sesame seeds, toasted until deep golden brown, then cooled
2 tablespoons sake
2 tablespoons soy sauce
1 tablespoon mirin
1 tablespoon caster (superfine) sugar
¼ teaspoon sesame oil
¼ teaspoon rice vinegar
800 g (1 lb 12 oz) fresh spinach, washed well

SERVES 2

30 g (1 oz) butter, melted
70 g (2¼ oz) fresh cod's roe (or roe of pollock, haddock or similar), eggs only, with membranes removed
4 tablespoon single (light) cream
1 tablespoon soy sauce
½ teaspoon dashi powder
200–250 g (7–9 oz) spaghetti
a couple pinches of shredded nori

METHOD

Grind the sesame seeds to a coarse, sandy powder using a mortar and pestle or spice grinder. In a separate bowl, stir together the sake, soy sauce, mirin, sugar, sesame oil and vinegar until the sugar dissolves. Prepare a large pan of boiling water, and a large bowl or container full of ice water. Blanch the spinach for 1 minute until just tender and deep green, then remove and plunge into the ice water to stop the cooking. Drain again and gently squeeze out any excess water.

Mix the drained and squeezed spinach with the sauce and half the ground sesame seeds. Serve with the remaining sesame sprinkled on top.

METHOD

Mix together the butter, roe, cream, soy sauce and dashi powder in a large bowl. Boil the pasta until al dente, then drain, but don't drain it too well – you'll need a little bit of the pasta water to help bind the sauce. Tip the hot pasta into the bowl with the sauce and mix well. Serve with a sprinkling of shredded nori on each portion.

東京の家庭料理

CUCUMBER AND WAKAME SUNOMONO

FRESH VINEGAR SALAD

Sunomono means 'vinegar thing', and like Carrot and Daikon Namasu (page 198), it's kind of a salad but also kind of a pickle. A pickle salad, maybe? Doesn't really matter, I guess. What does matter is that it's exceptionally refreshing and a particularly excellent accompaniment to oily fish.

MAKES 4 LITTLE SALADS, OR 8 TINY SALADS

25 g (1 oz) wakame
1 cucumber
big pinch of salt
100 ml (3½ fl oz/scant ½ cup) rice vinegar
25 g (1 oz/2 tablespoons) caster (superfine) sugar
15 g (½ oz) piece of ginger root, peeled and
    finely shredded
a few strips of lemon, lime or yuzu zest (optional)

METHOD

Rehydrate the wakame in cold water for about 30 minutes, then drain well. Slice the cucumber as thinly as you can (use a mandoline if you have one), then massage the salt into the cucumbers and leave to sit for 20 minutes to tenderise. Rinse the cucumbers under cold running water and squeeze out any excess water. Meanwhile, stir together the vinegar, sugar, ginger and citrus zest (if using) until the sugar dissolves. Toss the cucumber and wakame in the vinegar dressing. You can serve this immediately but it is perhaps more delicious after a few hours in the fridge, so the veg absorbs the dressing.

東
京
の
家
庭
料
理

OCHAZUKE

RICE AND FISH WITH TEA-INFUSED DASHI

Ochazuke is a Japanese home cooking staple, but you'll also encounter refined versions at traditional Japanese restaurants. Rice often completes a Japanese meal, and is typically found as one of the final courses in a traditional kaiseki meal, along with miso soup, and often followed by green tea to contribute a feeling of refreshment as well as satisfaction, like everything is being smoothly digested. Ochazuke combines all three – rice, soup and tea all in one. This is especially nice when you're feeling under the weather, as it is simultaneously invigorating and comforting.

SERVES 4

200 g (7 oz/1 cup) rice
500 ml (17 fl oz/2 cups) dashi
1 tablespoon loose green tea leaves or 2 green tea bags (I like genmai tea for this, but any will do)
1 tablespoon mirin
sea salt, to taste
150 g (5 oz) fish, cut into small pieces (any fish will do but something quite flavourful is best, like sea bass, bream, salmon or tuna)
2 teaspoons sesame seeds
12 g (¼ oz) sakura-ebi (tiny dried prawns (shrimp)) (optional)
4 teaspoons *bubu arare* or crushed *senbei*
1½ sheet of nori, cut into thin strips (or a few pinches of kizami-nori)

METHOD

Cook the rice according to the instructions on page 26. Bring the dashi, tea and mirin to a low simmer, then pass through a sieve to remove the tea. Taste and season as you like it (it should not be salty, but you will need a bit to boost the flavour of the dashi and subdue any potential bitterness from the tea.) To serve, place the rice into bowls, and top with the raw fish, sesame seeds, sakura-ebi (if using), bubu arare and nori. Just before serving, pour the hot dashi-tea mixture on top of the fish, ensuring that the fish has been lightly poached in the process.

東
京
の
家
庭
料
理

CARROT AND DAIKON NAMASU

LIGHTLY PICKLED SALAD

This simple dish is kind of a salad and kind of a pickle, perhaps most commonly found in special New Year's bento – red and white are considered auspicious colours, and growers in Japan even produce special blood-red carrots specifically for the occasion. But orange is close enough, I guess. This is a super-refreshing and super-easy little side, at home in any lunchbox or as a light counterpart to meaty dinners.

198

MAKES 8 TINY PORTIONS (FOR BENTO)
OR 4 SMALL SIDE DISHES

12-cm (4½-in) chunk of daikon, peeled
1 large-ish carrot (about 100–120 g (3½–4oz)), peeled
10 g (½ oz) kombu (about a 10-cm (4-in) square),
    rehydrated or left over from making Dashi
    (page 184)
big pinch of salt
1 tablespoon caster (superfine) sugar
3 tablespoons rice vinegar
a few strips of yuzu zest or lemon zest

METHOD

Cut the daikon and carrot into thin strips about 1 cm (½ in) wide and 2 mm (⅛ in) thick. Slice the kombu into very thin shreds. Combine the kombu with the veg, sprinkle them with salt and massage it into them, then leave to sit for about 20 minutes to tenderise.

Meanwhile, stir together the sugar, vinegar and yuzu zest or lemon zest. Squeeze any excess liquid out from the veg, then toss the vegetables in the vinegar dressing. Taste and add salt as needed. This can be enjoyed straight away, but it is best after about an hour in the fridge to soak up some of the dressing.

東
京
の
家
庭
料
理

At Home in Tokyo

FRIED RICE WITH SALMON SCRAPS

200

Japanese supermarkets often sell off-cuts of salmon or other large fish because resourceful home cooks know that there's great flavour to be found in the bits of fish flesh that cling to the bones and skin. You might be surprised at how much delicious, useful meat you can get off the carcass of a salmon, and while it obviously isn't the same as having a big, meaty grilled fillet or tidy slices of sashimi, there's still loads you can do with it: stuff it into onigiri, work it through a creamy pasta sauce, add it to Ochazuke (page 197) or miso soup, or use it in fried rice – my favourite! Salmon scraps have loads of flavour and fat that renders out to coat each grain of rice, so every mouthful is full of salmony goodness. (This is excellent combined with Kitopiro Chahan, by the way, page 140.)

SERVES 4

1 small salmon carcass (you can use a fish you
    cleaned yourself, or ask your fishmonger –
    often they'll give you salmon bones for free)
1 tablespoon oil
1 onion, diced
1 carrot, peeled and diced
4 eggs
4 spring onions (scallions), cut into
    1-cm (½-in) chunks
150 g (5 oz) peas (frozen is fine)
500 g (1 lb 2 oz/2½ cups) cooked rice (from 250 g
    (9 oz/2¼ cups) uncooked); chilled overnight,
    if possible
2 tablespoons soy sauce
1 tablespoon sake
1 tablespoon mirin
½ tablespoon sesame oil
½ teaspoon dashi powder
white pepper, to taste
40 g (1½ oz) ikura (optional)

METHOD

Scrape as much meat and fat from the salmon bones as you can – I find it easiest to use a small spoon for this. You might end up with more meat than you need, so save any excess, cook it, and use it as you would tinned tuna.

Heat the oil in a frying pan (skillet) over a medium heat, add the onion and carrot and cook until softened slightly. Add the salmon scraps and cook for a few minutes so some of the fat renders out. Add the eggs and scramble them in the pan, then add the spring onions, peas, rice, soy sauce, sake, mirin, sesame oil, dashi powder and pepper. Stir-fry to combine, making sure you break up any big clumps of rice as you go. Serve in bowls with the ikura on top.

東
京
の
家
庭
料
理

TERIYAKI TOFU AND HIJIKI PATTIES

GANMODOKI

Variations on these little tofu 'burgers' are found
all over the place in Japan – sometimes on restaurant
menus, sometimes in home kitchens, and frequently
in bento. The *hijiki* and shiitake have a lovely strong,
meaty flavour, so they're a nice way to make tofu
taste a bit more flavourful and substantial. They're
very easy to make AND they're VEGAN! Woooooo
vegan!

204

MAKES 12 PATTIES

5 dried shiitake (about 12 g/½ oz)
10 g (½ oz) dried hijiki seaweed
200 ml (7 fl oz/scant 1 cup) hot water
4 tablespoons soy sauce
2 tablespoons mirin
2 tablespoons sake
2 tablespoons caster (superfine) sugar
1 tablespoon ketchup
½ tablespoon cornflour (cornstarch), mixed with
    a little cold water
400 g (14 oz/1 block) firm cotton tofu
40 g (1½ oz/⅔ cup) panko, or more as needed
2 garlic cloves, finely grated
15 g (½ oz) piece of ginger root, peeled
    and finely grated
1 small carrot, peeled and grated
2 spring onions (scallions) or nira, finely sliced
1 tablespoon white sesame seeds
big pinch of salt and white pepper
oil, for shallow frying (at least 2 tablespoons)

METHOD

Cover the shiitake and hijiki in the hot water and leave
to rehydrate for 20–30 minutes. When the mushrooms
are fully rehydrated and soft, drain and squeeze them
out, reserving the liquid. Finely chop the mushrooms.

Combine the soy sauce, mirin, sake, sugar, ketchup
and 2 tablespoons of the shiitake-hijiki liquid in a
small saucepan. Bring to a low boil, then whisk in the
cornflour slurry. Boil for a few minutes to thicken,
stirring continuously, then remove from the heat.

Break up the tofu into small crumbles with your hand
or a fork. Add the shiitake, hijiki, panko, garlic, ginger,
carrot, spring onions or nira, sesame seeds, salt and
white pepper and mix well, mashing the tofu into a kind
of paste. Leave for 5 minutes or so for the panko to
absorb the liquid in the mixture – it should form a sort
of thick, moist, dough-like consistency. If the mixture
is too wet, add more panko. Form this mixture into
12 small patties, 7 cm (2¾ in) across and 1.5 cm
(⅔ in) thick.

Pour a generous layer of oil in the bottom of a frying
pan (skillet) and place on high heat. Fry the patties until
deep brown on each side, then remove and transfer
to a baking tray. Top each one with a spoonful of the
teriyaki sauce and grill on high for a few minutes so
that the glaze fuses with the patties and caramelises
slightly (if you have extra sauce, you can serve it on the
side as a dip). Serve with salad, rice and miso soup for
a main meal, or keep in the fridge for bento (these are
delicious cold).

東京の家庭料理

CALAMARI TEMPURA

How do you get the seafood-phobic to eat squid?
Deep-fry it, of course. Calamari is always a bar-snack
favourite, but it's even nicer when given the tempura
treatment – light and crisp and as easy to eat as
popcorn. You'll find these in both home kitchens and
izakaya in Tokyo and they are excellent fodder for
sake or beer.

MAKES A VERY LARGE AMOUNT – CERTAINLY
ENOUGH FOR 4, MAYBE ENOUGH FOR 8

200 g (7 oz/scant 1⅔ cups) plain (all-purpose) flour
100 g (3½ oz/heaped ¾ cup) cornflour (cornstarch)
1 tablespoon aonori
¼ teaspoon salt
1 egg
400 ml (13 fl oz/generous 1½ cups) very cold
    sparkling water
600 g (1 lb 5 oz) squid rings
about 1.5 litres (52 fl oz/6 cups) oil, for deep-frying
1 lemon, quartered
125 g (4 oz) mayonnaise

METHOD

Heat the oil in a very wide, deep pan to 190°C (375°F). If
you don't have a thermometer, simply drip a few drops
of the batter into the oil to test it. If the batter sinks, it's
too cold. If the batter immediately floats and sizzles, it's
too hot. If the batter sinks just below the surface of the
oil, then rises up and start to sizzle, it should be perfect.

Mix together the flours, aonori and salt – ensure the
flours are well combined or the batter will be difficult
to mix. Beat the egg, then mix with the sparkling water.
Add the dry mixture to the wet mixture and mix just
until the batter comes together and is the consistency
of double cream – it should still be slightly lumpy. It's
a good idea to mix the batter with chopsticks so the
gluten in the flour isn't worked too much as it's mixed.

Dredge the squid rings in the batter, let some of the
excess batter drip off, then carefully drop them into
the hot oil. Fry until barely golden and hard to the touch
(feel them as they fry with chopsticks or tongs). You
will probably have to do this in batches, in which case
you can just eat them as they come out and then go
back and fry some more. Drain on paper towels and
serve immediately or keep them hot in an oven set to
60–70°C (140–160°F/gas ¼), or as low as your oven will
go, with the door slightly open to let the moisture out.
Serve with lemon wedges and mayo on the side.

東
京
の
家
庭
料
理

MENCHI KATSU

BREADED AND FRIED MINCED MEAT PATTIES

208

Since they're based on minced (ground) meat, *menchi katsu* are one of the cheapest katsu around, making them extremely popular among students, families, and blue- and white-collar workers alike. They're sort of like a burger, sort of like a meatball, but possibly better than both because they're breaded and deep-fried. The panko shell locks in so much meaty juice, which then comes gushing out when you bite into them.

You will also need a probe thermometer.

MAKES 8 MENCHI

For the burgers
50 g (2 oz/heaped ¾ cup) panko
2 egg yolks
4 tablespoons double (heavy) cream
250 g (9 oz) minced (ground) beef
250 g (9 oz) minced (ground) pork
1 leek, diced
50 g (2 oz) shiitake mushrooms, de-stemmed
    and finely chopped
pinch of freshly grated nutmeg (optional)
salt and black pepper
handful of fresh parsley, finely chopped

For cooking
oil, for deep-frying
60 g (2 oz/½ cup) plain (all-purpose) flour
2 eggs, beaten with a splash of water or milk
80 g (3 oz/1⅓ cups) panko
tonkatsu sauce or ketchup

METHOD

To make the burgers, combine the panko, egg yolks and cream, and leave to soak until the panko has absorbed the liquid and become soft. Combine this with the beef, pork, leek, mushrooms, nutmeg (if using), salt, pepper and parsley and mix well. Form the mixture into 8 balls, then slap the balls back and forth between your hands several times (this will help make the patties more dense and air-free, which makes them less likely to break open while frying). Flatten each ball into a patty about 2 cm (¾ in) thick.

Heat the oil to 160°C (320°F). Dredge each patty in the flour, then the beaten egg, then the panko. Fry for about 8 minutes, or less if you'd like these a little pink in the middle. Serve with rice and gallons and gallons of tonkatsu sauce or ketchup.

東
京
の
家
庭
料
理

MICROWAVE CHAWANMUSHI

STEAMED DASHI CUSTARD CUPS

Chawanmushi are little cups of savoury egg custard studded with hidden jewels of deliciousness, like chicken or prawns (shrimp) or mushrooms or gingko nuts. I love them, but I used to despise them. I first tried them not in big Tokyo but in Little Tokyo, in Los Angeles, where I'd visit Japanese restaurants and order more or less randomly, partly to try new things but also partly because I didn't know what the hell anything was. I first had chawanmushi as part of a set meal, and it very nearly made me retch – I was wholly unprepared for something that felt like flan but tasted like fish. Hey, now there's an idea: fish flan! Hashtag foodtrends2019 etc.

I don't know how but I ultimately overcame my disgust, but now chawanmushi is among my favourite traditional Japanese dishes. They always seemed like too much of a faff to make at home, what with needing a big steamer set-up, but then I learned from my mother-in-law that you can make them in the microwave. GAME CHANGER – especially if your home kitchen, like many in Tokyo, has limited space and cooking equipment. Microwave chawanmushi are just as delicately textured as steamed versions, but so much easier. They're a super side dish to have with just about any traditional Japanese meal.

MAKES 4 CHAWANMUSHI

2 eggs
360 ml (12½ fl oz/1½ cups) dashi
1 teaspoon soy sauce
½ teaspoon salt
1 grilled or poached chicken thigh, cut into
    8 little pieces
2 shiitake mushrooms, destemmed and thinly sliced
5 cm (2 in) piece of carrot, peeled and sliced about
    2 mm (⅛ in) thick
4 raw prawns (shrimp), peeled and deveined
60 g (2 oz) shelled edamame or 8 sugar snap peas,
    halved
4 leaves of mitsuba or parsley (optional)

METHOD

Whisk the eggs, dashi, soy sauce and salt together until very smooth. Place 2 pieces of chicken, a few slices of shiitake and carrot, 1 prawn, and some beans or snap peas in the bottom of 4 lidded, heatproof chawan bowls or ramekins. Pour the egg mixture into each container. If your bowls have lids, use those; if you're using ramekins, cover them in cling film (plastic wrap).

Place the bowls or ramekins in a microwave-safe tray or dish and pour in about 2.5 cm (1 in) of boiling water around them. Place in the microwave and cook on high for anywhere between 1 and 5 minutes – it all depends on the microwave, so start with 1 minute, check them, then keep cooking in 15-second increments until the egg has just set. Overcooking them will result in something like scrambled eggs or egg drop soup, which isn't so bad, but it's not what we're going for.

When the eggs are set, garnish with the mitsuba or parsley and leave to cool slightly before serving.

東
京
の
家
庭
料
理

STIR-FRIED LOTUS ROOT WITH PORK AND CHILLI BEAN PASTE

Some dishes in Tokyo are both exotic restaurant cooking and humdrum home cooking, all depending on context. Something like this lotus root stir-fry could be either fine Chinese cuisine or a school lunch, depending on who made it and what goes into it. Trends in Tokyo move so fast you can actually see foods go from novel restaurant dishes to home cooking staples in a matter of years. I suppose this dish is based on Sichuan cookery, which was once the domain of Chinese restaurants. Thanks to the availability and rising popularity of Chinese ingredients and recipes, Sichuan-inspired cookery is now within any Tokyo home cook's grasp. Its primary seasoning is the particularly popular *doubanjiang*, a fermented Sichuan broad bean and chilli paste that tastes kind of like a funky, spicy, salty miso.

SERVES 4

2 tablespoons vegetable oil
1 onion, thinly sliced
250 g (9 oz) minced (ground) pork
60 g (2 oz) doubanjiang
300 g (10½ oz) lotus root, washed and peeled,
    then halved and sliced into 3-mm (⅛-in) thick
    half-rounds (you can use frozen lotus root)
1 green pepper, cut into 1 cm (½ in) strips
15 g (½ oz) piece of ginger root, peeled and julienned
2 garlic cloves, thinly sliced
2 tablespoons sake
1 tablespoon caster (superfine) sugar
½ tablespoon cornflour (cornstarch), mixed with
    2 tablespoons water
½ teaspoon white sesame seeds, toasted until deep
    golden brown

METHOD

Heat the oil in a wok or frying pan (skillet) over a high heat, then add the onion and cook until starting to brown. Add the pork mince and stir-fry until browned, breaking it up so that no large chunks remain. Add the doubanjiang, lotus root, pepper, ginger and garlic, and continue to stir-fry until the lotus root is just tender – still firm but not crunchy. Add the sake and sugar, then the cornflour slurry, stirring as you go. Cook for a few more minutes until the sauce has thickened and coated the veg. Sprinkle with sesame seeds and serve with rice.

東京の家庭料理

SOUPED UP
INSTANT RAMEN

Instant ramen: not a proper meal. Nutritionally speaking, you're looking at flour in fatty salt water, maybe with a few bits of freeze-dried vegetables. And that's fine! Sometimes the hot hit of MSG and carbs from a Cup Noodle is all you need. But actually, basic instant ramen provides an excellent platform on which to build something truly delicious; even bad instant ramen tastes good, but it lacks the mouthfeel and variety of textures and flavours of real ramen. Luckily, those things are easy to prep and to add, transforming this humble snack into a satisfying meal.

SERVES 1

1 egg
2 tablespoons soy sauce (optional)
1 tablespoon mirin (optional)
some fresh greens such as spinach or chopped
    cabbage, and/or bean sprouts
1 cup/bowl/package instant ramen
some kind of flavourful fat – lard, bacon fat, sesame
    oil, chilli oil, butter, chicken fat, etc. (optional)
something pickled – bamboo shoots, beni shoga,
    pickled mustard greens, kimchi, etc.
a few slices roasted pork, ham or chicken (optional)
1 spring onion (scallion), finely sliced

METHOD

Bring a pan of water to a rolling boil, carefully lower in the egg, and cook for 6½ minutes. Remove the egg and transfer to a bowl of cold water and leave to cool completely (change the water once or twice if it starts to warm up). Peel the egg and, if you are so inclined and you have the time, marinate it in the soy sauce and mirin for at least an hour. Blanch the greens in boiling water until just tender, then prepare the instant ramen according to the instructions on the package. Garnish the ramen with the fat (if using), the egg, greens, pickles, meat and spring onion, if you like.

東
京
の
家
庭
料
理

5F
4F
3F
2F
1F
B1F
B2F

FRESH TOFU FROM SCRATCH

One of the delights of life in Tokyo is finding all the little local shops that specialise in certain foods, often everyday items made with care – things like pickles, sweets or fresh bread. But perhaps my favourite thing to buy from neighbourhood shops is freshly made, just-set tofu. Making it takes effort, but it's worth it for the sublime flavour of barely set, still-warm tofu.

216

MAKES ABOUT 900 G (2 LB) TOFU

You will need a few utensils:
a blender
a big pot – should be at least 6 litres (210 fl oz)
    if you have one, but 4 litres (140 fl oz) will do
a big container (about 4 litres (140 fl oz)
a colander, perforated tray or tofu press
a flat plate, lid or board that fits into your colander
    or tray
a slotted spoon (or another, smaller colander)
a spatula
a sieve
muslin (cheesecloth)
something big and heavy, like a brick or a jar
    of pickles

300 g (10½ oz) dried soybeans
3.5 litres (122 fl oz/13½ cups) plus 180 ml
    (6½ fl oz/¾ cup) water, plus more for soaking
8 g (½ oz) salt
18 g (¾ oz) nigari (tofu coagulant salts) or Epsom salts

METHOD

Soak the beans with about three times their volume of water. They need at least 8 hours, so overnight is best. Drain the beans, then purée them with some of the 3.5 litres (122 fl oz/13½ cups) of water in your blender. You'll have to do this in batches, and be mindful that the mixture will froth up quite a lot, so don't fill the blender more than two-thirds full. Get the mixture as smooth as possible – leave it blending for at least a minute. Add the bean purée along with any extra water to your pot. This is your soy milk.

Bring the soy milk to a very gentle simmer – don't boil it! If your soy milk boils, it won't affect the outcome of your tofu, but it almost definitely will boil over. If you're a food science geek, you'll already know that soy lecithin is an excellent foaming agent. So unless your pot is really, really big, don't let the milk boil or you will have a

lot of mopping up to do. Gently simmer the soy milk for about 20 minutes; this is to cook out the beans' protein, and the aroma will go from a starchy, grassy, raw green bean-like smell to a sweet, cake-batter like smell.

Line the colander with the muslin and perch it over a big container. Ladle or pour the soy milk into it. When the dripping slows, work it with a spatula. Eventually you'll end up with a fibrous pulp. Keep pressing down on this pulp to extract the milk or, if it's not too hot, bundle the muslin around it and squeeze it out like a sponge. The resulting dry matter is called *okara*. It's actually quite useful and *crazy* healthy, with tons of fibre and protein. Save it and put it into baked goods, or use it to thicken sauces and dressings. Pour the strained soy milk back into the pot and add the salt. Stir the nigari into the 180 ml (6½ fl oz/¾ cup) water until it dissolves completely, then add this solution to the soy milk and stir a few times, then leave it to stand for 5 minutes to let the proteins coagulate.

Meanwhile, prepare your press: you can use a colander or a perforated tray or, better yet, a tofu press. It's a pretty arcane piece of kit but, if you love tofu and plan to make a lot of it, it's invaluable. I got mine on eBay. Line with muslin and perch it over another container to catch the whey as it drips out. Scoop out the coagulated soy milk and veg with a slotted spoon or a small colander. Tilt and gently shake the spoon to drain off excess liquid, then place the curds into your press. Carry on doing this until you've separated all the curds. When the globules get too small then switch to a sieve.

At this point, you could just let the curds drain and set, dish them out, and enjoy still warm, with a splash of soy sauce or tsuyu and sesame seeds. This is one of the finest, most ethereal tofu experiences one can have.

But if you want firmer tofu, or you're saving it for later, weigh down the curds with a plate or lid or board with something heavy on top of it so that all the extra moisture is pressed out. Wait for an hour or so. At this point, your tofu should be just firm enough to remove from the press and slice. If you want it even firmer, just leave it in the press for another hour. Keep the finished tofu covered in the fridge for up to 4 days.

東京の家庭料理

**FIVE IN THE MORNING:
RISE WITH THE SUN TO VISIT
TSUKIJI MARKET!**

**WITH WHITE GLOVES RAISED UP;
A KIND SMILE, AND A WHISTLE
'NO VISITORS PLEASE!'**

**OH WELL – WE CAN STILL
GET SOME MIGHTY FINE SUSHI**

TOKYO

5

KABOCHA カボチャ

MODERN

F

YUZU ユズ

5

F

TOKYO MODERN

JAPANESE REGIONAL CUISINE
IN THE CAPITAL

Japan doesn't always live up to its image. Kyoto, for example, is often portrayed as some kind of holdover from pre-modern Japan, a quaint city of serene teahouses, beautiful temples, refined food and elegant geisha (so many geisha). But most of Kyoto isn't like that at all. It's a massive city of 1.5 million, smelly and dirty and crowded. It's horrendously humid and rainy in the summer, surprisingly run-down in places and just plain boring in others, and increasingly touristy. And I'm saying this as someone who likes Kyoto. It just does not live up to expectations.

Tokyo is the opposite. Tokyo doesn't just live up to expectations, it exceeds them by leaps and bounds. I knew Tokyo would be super-modern, but I really wasn't prepared for just how far they've really run with modernity there. I expected lots of bright lights and arcades and vending machines and cool trains - and Tokyo delivered in spades, along with the world's most impressive toilets, insane street fashions, cafés where you can hang out with owls and otters and robots - actual robots. It really is incredible. And, of course, there are chefs and bartenders who also contribute to the hypermodernity of Tokyo, often by combining new ideas from around the globe with clever nods to Japan's own history and culture.

UMEBOSHI MARTINI

PICKLED PLUM MARTINI

Some of Tokyo's most modern fare actually comes in liquid form. Cocktail culture has always been a big deal in Tokyo and, in the past few decades, a delightful trend has emerged for mixologists to create cocktails with the same level of exacting detail that often goes into something like sushi, combined with new technology and techniques that have arisen out of the global modernist cocktail movement. Many of these are tricky to replicate at home, but a simple, elegant and unusual neo-Tokyo cocktail you can try is the umeboshi martini. A sort of riff on a classic dirty martini, this bracing cocktail combines the intense salty-sour flavour of umeboshi with a crisp and clean classic martini base.

MAKES 1 COCKTAIL

25 ml (2 tablespoons) gin
25 ml (2 tablespoons) vodka
10 ml (2 teaspoons) umeshu
10 ml (2 teaspoons) Lillet rosé (or dry vermouth)
5 ml (1 teaspoon) sweet vermouth
2 umeboshi
ice cubes

METHOD

Combine all the liquours in a shaker with one of the umeboshi and muddle to break up the umeboshi. Add ice cubes and shake for a minute until very cold. Place the other umeboshi in a very well-chilled cocktail glass and strain the cocktail over it.

TOMATO COCKTAIL

One of the most unique cocktail bars in Tokyo is Gen Yamamoto, named for its auteur bartender who has applied the *kaiseki* ethos of showcasing top-quality, seasonal produce to make exquisitely crafted cocktails, which are served as short tasting menus. These menus vary frequently, and always name-check where the produce comes from: potatoes from Hokkaido, perhaps, or corn from Gunma, or peaches from Yamanashi. The result is gorgeous cocktails that beautifully capture the essence of the featured produce. Some of his most famous creations are based on tomato, used in both fresh and cooked forms to express both their sweet, tart, fruity side and their deep, rich, umami side. Obviously I have no idea what his exact recipes are, but this is a reasonably good approximation of a Yamamoto-style tomato cocktail.

MAKES 1 COCKTAIL

2 medium-sized tomatoes (about 50–60 g (2 oz) each), strictly the best, in-season tomatoes you can get
1 shiso leaf, cut in half lengthways; or 2 basil leaves
60 ml (2 fl oz/¼ cup) very good-quality rice shochu
cracked ice
large ice cube

METHOD

Remove the core from each tomato and cut one of them in half. Place the cut tomato in an oven set to 100°C (212°F), or as low as your oven will go, and bake for about 3 hours until shrivelled and concentrated. Finely chop both tomatoes and transfer to a shaker with half of the shiso leaf – or 1 basil leaf, if using – and muddle well. Add the shochu and a handful of cracked ice, then shake well. Strain through a fine sieve into a tumbler or flute over one large ice cube. Garnish with the other half of the shiso leaf, or 1 basil leaf, if using.

Where to find
Gen Yamamoto
Azabu Juban, 〒106-0045, genyamamoto.jp

東京モダン

−25°C MOJITO

Some trendy Tokyo cocktail bars have taken
to serving frozen cocktails – but not the fruity
fluorescent kind like you might find at a Caribbean
resort. These are proper cocktails, well-made using
fine spirits and mixers, simply frozen down (−25°C/
−13°F is always the advertised temperature, for some
reason) so they are bracingly clean and refreshing,
but their flavours blossom and develop beautifully
on the palate as they warm up in your mouth. Many
classic cocktails (or pure spirits) are given this
treatment around Tokyo, but my favourite is probably
the mojito – the mint and lime works wonderfully
frozen down, a perfect sharpener on a cold and
drizzly Tokyo evening, or a perfect refresher on
a hot and muggy Tokyo day.

226

MAKES 10 LITTLE COCKTAILS,
TO BE KEPT IN THE FREEZER

40–50 fresh mint leaves
4 limes, cut into wedges
5 tablespoons demerara sugar
400 ml (13 fl oz/generous 1½ cups) good-quality rum
cracked ice

METHOD

Clap the mint leaves between your hands to release
their aroma, then place in a shaker with the lime and
sugar. Muddle until the limes are pulverised, then add
the rum and continue to muddle until the sugar is
dissolved. Add a handful of cracked ice and shake for
a few minutes, then strain through a sieve. Pour into a
bottle and transfer to the freezer until very, very cold
(most freezers won't get down to −25°C, but don't
worry – it just has to be extremely cold). Serve in
50 ml (1¾ fl oz/3 tablespoons) measures in small,
chilled glasses.

東京モダン

Where to find
Bar Kokage バーコカゲ Akasaka-Mitsuke, 〒107-0052

AT MITSUKOSHI
I SPEND HOURS PERUSING
THE MARVELLOUS FOOD!

I EAT FRUIT, SUSHI,
GYOZA, AND TONKATSU, TOO;
THEN, I NEED A REST

AND LUCKILY, THERE'S
NO NEED FOR EMBARRASSMENT:

THE SOUND OF WATER!

YUZU-MARINATED OLIVES

I love to slum it, and when I travel I'm generally more than happy to just stick to street food and dive bars. Hell, in Tokyo I could probably just eat ramen all the time. But even I do like a touch of class every now and then, and that's when it's time to head to the New York Bar on the 52nd floor of the Park Hyatt hotel in Shinjuku. Cinephiles will already know this iconic bar from *Lost in Translation* as the venue where Bill Murray and Scarlett Johansson quaffed cocktails and flirted surreptitiously in futile attempts to curb their pitiful bourgeois ennui. Like, why so emo, guys?! Just sit back, enjoy the smooth jazz, enjoy the stunning views, enjoy the exquisite ¥2,000 cocktails, and enjoy some classic bar snacks with clever and subtle Japanese flavours, like these simple and delicious yuzu-marinated olives.

2 tablespoons yuzu juice
1 tablespoon good olive oil
¼ teaspoon yuzu-kosho or finely chopped yuzu peel (optional)
200 g (7 oz) very good-quality olives (I like kalamata or nocellara for this)

METHOD

Stir together the yuzu juice, olive oil and yuzu-kosho or yuzu peel. Toss the olives with this mixture and leave to marinate in the fridge for at least 1 hour. Enjoy with JAZZ and a MARTINI.

東
京
モ
ダ
ン

```
Where to find

New York Bar
Shinjuku, 〒160-0023, tokyo.park.hyatt.co.jp
```

'DENTUCKY' FRIED CHICKEN

STUFFED AND FRIED CHICKEN WINGS

230

One of Tokyo's most celebrated young chefs is Zaiyu Hasegawa, who since 2007 has been delighting customers with his playful and creative takes on the classic kaiseki format. While some of his dishes are made and presented in a fairly traditional style, others subvert expectations in a variety of novel ways. There is, for example, his foie gras *monaka* – a rice wafer sandwich that usually contains sweet red bean paste, instead hiding a rich liver parfait, guava compote and white miso. But perhaps his most famous, most show-stopping piece is his Dentucky Fried Chicken, which comes packaged in a cardboard KFC-style box. It contains delicately crispy fried chicken wings that have been meticulously deboned and stuffed with surprising flavours, which can include red rice, burdock, lotus root, cashews and goji berries. These little morsels of chicken joy are something other chefs might present more formally or stoically, so the diner is forced to appreciate the time and technique that went into them. Not so at Den, where the KFC presentation makes the whole experience lighter and more fun, a bit like opening a present on Christmas morning (indeed, having KFC on Christmas is apparently a cherished tradition in Hasegawa's family). Kaiseki is often practised like a kind of sombre religion, and while it's rarely short of beautiful, it's almost never as fun as it is at Den.

Hasegawa changes the filling of his stuffed wings frequently, sometimes based on flavours found in other Japanese classic dishes, so I fill mine with a mixture based on one of my favourite foods: gyoza.

You'll need a probe thermometer for this dish.

MAKES 16 WINGS, ENOUGH FOR 8 PEOPLE
EATING AT DEN OR 2 REGULAR PEOPLE

16 chicken wings, mid-joint and wingtip only (if you can't get them like this, buy them whole, chop the first joint off and save it for another recipe)
100 g (3½ oz) shiitake mushrooms, destemmed and diced
2 large Chinese cabbage leaves, finely diced
60 g (2 oz) bamboo shoots, diced
20 g (¾ oz) garlic, finely chopped or grated
15 g (½ oz) piece of ginger root, peeled and finely grated
¼ teaspoon sesame oil
¼ teaspoon truffle oil
10 g (½ oz) chicken fat or lard
½ teaspoon salt
¼ teaspoon white pepper
250 g (9 oz) minced (ground) pork
1 egg white
1 tablespoon soy sauce
100 g (3½ oz) potato starch
oil, for deep-frying

METHOD

Using a thin knife, carefully remove the bones from the chicken wings. Do this by inserting the knife along one side of the bone and gently working it around the bone using a back-and-forth wiggling and scraping motion. When the bones are loose from the flesh, grip them with a clean cloth and break the joint, then firmly pull the bones out to create a cavity in the wing.

Sauté the mushrooms, cabbage, bamboo shoots, garlic and ginger in the oils and fat along with the salt and pepper until the mushrooms have softened and the cabbage has lost most of its water and has begun to colour. Remove from the heat and leave to cool, then mix into the pork. Stuff a little ball of mince mixture into each boned-out chicken wing, then seal the ends by weaving a cocktail stick (toothpick) through them. Puncture each side of the wing with a cocktail stick or the tip of a small, sharp knife.

Heat the oil to 180°C (350°F). Beat the egg white with the soy sauce and brush this onto the surface of each wing, ensuring they're evenly coated. Dip the brushed wings in the potato starch, then fry for about 6 minutes until the internal temperature is at least 75°C (170°F) and it is golden brown. Drain on paper towels and leave to cool slightly before serving.

東京モダン

Where to find
Den 傳
Gaiemmae, 〒150-0001, jimbochoden.com

LES SAISONS-STYLE FOIE GRAS WITH STRAWBERRIES

In 2008 I went to Tokyo with my girlfriend (now wife) Laura, to meet her parents (eek) and have a generally awesome time as a young, drunken idiot let loose in the greatest city in the world. Laura's parents are modest people, but when they travel they really go for it. My mother-in-law, Emiko, in particular, books tables at some of the best restaurants she can find and seems to plan the rest of the trip around those bookings. And, luckily for us, we got to accompany her and my father-in-law to several of them. We ate fantastically well on that trip, but the meal I remember most fondly was at the French restaurant Les Saisons in the Imperial Hotel, notably designed by Frank Lloyd Wright. The chef was (and still is) Thierry Voisin, a seriously accomplished French chef who builds his dishes on a solid foundation of nouvelle cuisine, but with just enough modern flourishes to deliver plates that really wow. And the wowing-est plate of all was a dish I had of seared foie gras with strawberries and 25-year-old balsamic vinegar. To be honest, it didn't sound all that amazing when I ordered it – I mainly got it because I'd never really had foie gras before, except in a parfait at a restaurant in Hong Kong. But that set me up for one of the most profound culinary shocks of my entire life.

The foie gras was like nothing I had ever tasted before. It was like eating softened butter, or a warm custard of heavy cream, encased in a carbonised, perfectly firm skin; it was solid and structured, and yet the way it melted upon my tongue suggested Swiss milk chocolate. The flavour was unfathomably deep: silky, mellow, fatty sweetness washed over the inherent earthiness of liver. With the tang of the vinegar and the sweetness of the perfectly cooked strawberries, the dish was superbly balanced and tremendously easy to eat.

In fact, it nearly made me weep. And I believe that was the first time food ever made me feel that way.

SERVES 2

1 piece of white bread, crusts removed
20 g (¾ oz) butter, melted
30 g (1 oz/2 tablespoons) caster (superfine) sugar
1 tablespoon water
60 ml (2 fl oz/¼ cup) good-quality red wine vinegar
1 tablespoon red wine, not too tannic
seeds from ¼ vanilla pod
6 good strawberries, quartered
a little oil
about 160 g (5½ oz/4 slices) flash-frozen foie gras
salt and black pepper
a few drops very, very old balsamic vinegar
a few sprigs fresh chervil

233

METHOD

Preheat the oven to 150°C (300°F/gas 1). Roll out the bread into a wide, thin sheet, about 2 mm (⅛ in) thick. Cut the bread sheet in half, then cut one half into two strips and brush them on both sides with the melted butter, discarding the other half. Wrap each strip of bread around two 7-cm (3-in) ring moulds and bake for about 20 minutes, until golden brown. Leave to cool before carefully slipping each toast ring off the moulds.

Place the sugar and water in a saucepan and bring to the boil. Cook over a medium heat until the sugar becomes a golden caramel, then add the red wine vinegar. Bring to the boil and let the caramel dissolve, then add the red wine and vanilla seeds. Boil for a few minutes until reduced to a thin syrup. Add the strawberries and cook briefly until tender but not soft.

Heat the oil in a non-stick frying pan (skillet) over very high heat. Fry the foie gras in the oil for just a couple of minutes on each side, so it is nicely coloured but the inside doesn't start to melt. Rest the foie gras briefly on a kitchen cloth before plating, and season with salt and black pepper. To serve, spoon the strawberries and some of their sauce onto plates. Place the toast rings on their side on the plate, and rest the foie gras within the rings. Garnish with a few drops of balsamic vinegar here and there, and a few sprigs of fresh chervil on top of the foie gras.

東京モダン

Where to find
Les Saisons
Hibiya, 〒100-8558, imperialhotel.co.jp

RYUGIN-STYLE
STRAW-GRILLED PIGEON

234

One of Tokyo's most exquisite (and expensive) restaurants is Ryugin, captained by chef Seiji Yamamoto, who was once called the Japanese Heston Blumenthal due to his keen interest in food science and knack for theatrical presentation. You may have heard of some of his more outlandish methods, such as using a vintage Japanese woodblock printing apparatus to reproduce a newspaper review of the restaurant in edible squid ink sauce directly onto plates, or sending a hamo eel to get a CT scan so that he and his chefs could more accurately fillet this notoriously bony and difficult fish. But these kinds of unusual techniques aren't just for show, and ultimately what arrives on the plate is simply perfectly cooked and immaculately presented kaiseki dishes. He is also known for using under-utilised Japanese ingredients, including game. One of his signatures is a straw-grilled wild duck or pigeon dish, which is actually far more complicated than it appears. His dish uses every part of the bird, painstakingly broken down and carefully cooked to produce a little pigeon tsukune patty and a pigeon salad to accompany the grilled crown. I would not expect anyone to recreate this dish at home – I certainly can't – but how he prepares the pigeon to achieve a crisp skin, perfectly cooked centre, and a whiff of rustic smoke actually is do-able (if you have the time and ambition).

You will need a probe thermometer for this dish.

SERVES 2

2 crowns of wood pigeon, teal, mallard or similar
1 litre (34 fl oz/4 cups) vegetable oil with a very
    high smoke point, such as rapeseed (canola)
    or sunflower
salt and finely ground white pepper
handful of good-quality charcoal
handful of straw

METHOD

Carefully remove any bits of feather or down from the pigeon crowns. Use a blowtorch to lightly brown the skin and remove any remaining tiny bits of down, then thoroughly dry the surface of the bird with a hair dryer. Heat the oil to 230°C (445°F) in a large, wide, deep pot or deep-fryer. Hold each pigeon over the surface of the oil in a metal sieve or spider. Carefully ladle oil over the top of the crown 8–10 times, pausing for a moment between each ladle for the skin to cool and dry slightly, until it is taut and bronze in colour. Leave the pigeons to cool, and let the oil temperature fall to 55°C (130°F). Keeping the oil at that temperature, lower in the pigeons and leave them submerged in the oil for 40 minutes. Remove and drain well, patting the surface dry with paper towel, and leave to cool completely. Remove the breasts from the bone and thread each one onto skewers. Season the meat side of the breasts (not the skin) with salt and pepper.

Heat the charcoal to white-hot, set between two rows of bricks that should come up about 25 cm (10 in) above the top of the coals. Throw some straw on the top of the coals and rest the pigeon skewers on the bricks, above the straw. Grill skin-side down for a few minutes, until it has turned a rich brown colour. Place some more straw in a metal container with a lid and add a small piece of hot charcoal. Place the breasts in the container, away from the heat source, and place a lid on the pan. Leave for 10 minutes to smoke, then remove the breasts. Rest briefly, then slice and serve.

東
京
モ
ダ
ン

Where to find
Ryugin 日本料理龍吟
Hibiya, 〒100-0006, nihonryori-ryugin.com

COARSE CHICKEN LIVER PÂTÉ

Many yakitori chefs in Tokyo are taking the humble art of bird-firing into new frontiers of chickencraft, but they typically do so in ways that are subtle rather than showy. Instead of using scientific techniques or strange flourishes in presentation, they instead focus on how best to source and prepare everything that goes into their work: the best charcoal, how to heat said charcoal, how to create and control smoke throughout cooking, finding the best quality birds and carving them up with care. However, every now and again you will come across something you simply won't find at your average hole-in-the-wall yakitori joint. One of those things is chicken liver pâté, which can now be found on a few modern yakitori menus around Tokyo, though it is still quite the novelty. One thing that sets some of these pâtés apart from your typical European versions is that they are often served slightly warm, which is really lovely, maintaining the melt-in-the-mouth quality of freshly grilled liver. Accompaniments differ from shop to shop, but I've always thought chicken liver is perfect with the fleshy tang of Japanese plums.

SERVES 4

2 umeboshi, stoned and chopped
2 ripe plums, stoned, peeled and chopped
60 ml (2 fl oz/¼ cup) umeshu
40 g (1½ oz) duck fat (or better yet, chicken fat, if you have some)
2 banana shallots, finely diced
salt and pepper
2 tablespoons sake
400 g (14 oz) chicken livers, deveined
sansho and sea salt
½ baguette, sliced and toasted

METHOD

Combine the umeboshi, plums and umeshu in a saucepan and bring to the boil. Cook until reduced to a jam-like consistency, then leave to cool. Melt the fat in a frying pan (skillet) and add the shallots, salt and pepper. Cook over a medium heat until soft and slightly browned, then add the sake and leave to boil off completely. Thread the chicken livers onto skewers and grill over medium-hot coals with a handful of wood chips thrown in for about 10 minutes until smoky and charred on the outside but still pink in the middle. While still warm, chop the livers into a chunky paste, folding in the shallots and duck fat as you go. Shape the pâté into blocks or quenelles and garnish with a bit of sansho and sea salt. Serve with toasted baguette and the plum jam.

東京モダン

Where to find

Imai 今井
Gaiemmae, 〒150-0001, yakitoriimai.jp

LEMON SHIO RAMEN

Innovation in Tokyo isn't limited to top-floor hotel cocktail bars or Michelin-starred restaurants; quite the contrary, chefs in all strata of Tokyo dining are constantly experimenting, producing new takes on old classics all the time. One dish that's constantly being fiddled with and fussed over is ramen, and there's always something new to try in Tokyo's ramen scene. Sometimes nü-ramen options are just gimmicks, but more often they're earnest attempts to perfect a certain flavour or experience. One of my favourite recent trends in Tokyo ramen is the addition of citrus, popularised by the local ramen chain Afuri, where a light and clear broth is infused with the refreshing scent of yuzu. Other shops have done similar things, swapping the yuzu out for other citrus like *sudachi* or *kabosu*, but I think good old lemon works perfectly. Many people gravitate towards the rich and intense when they go out for ramen, but it's nice to discover that ramen can also be soothing and subtle. And that's the beauty of ramen – it can be just about anything you want it to be.

SERVES 4

For the broth

1.8 litres (60 fl oz/7½ cups) water
100 g (3½ oz) chicken feet
3 chicken backs
6 chicken wings (whole wings, not segments)
1 onion, quartered
100 g (3½ oz) ginger root, peeled and sliced
10 g (½ oz) kombu (about a 10-cm (4-in) square), rinsed
20 g (¾ oz) katsuobushi
1 lemon, thinly sliced (you will need 8 slices)

To serve

2 tablespoons good-quality mirin
2 tablespoons sea salt, or a little more or less, to taste
2 boneless and skinless chicken thighs
4 portions thin, straight ramen noodles (fresh is best)
50 g (2 oz) mizuna or similar fresh leafy greens, chopped
1 spring onion (scallion), finely sliced
a few grinds of black pepper
1 sheet of nori, cut into 4 squares

METHOD

To make the broth, combine the water, chicken feet, chicken backs, wings, onion and ginger in a large stock pot or casserole. Gradually bring to the boil over a medium heat, skimming the scum off the surface as it begins to bubble. Simmer for about half an hour, or until no new scum rises to the top, skimming constantly.

Meanwhile, preheat the oven to 120°C (250°F/ gas ¼). Top up the water to cover the bones, if needed, then cover with a lid or tin foil and transfer to the oven. Leave to simmer in the oven for 4 hours. Remove the bones, and pass the broth through a fine sieve. Add the kombu, katsuobushi and 4 lemon slices and leave to infuse for 1 hour. Pass through a sieve again and measure – you will need 1.4 litres (50 fl oz/6 cups) of broth in total, so top up with water as needed. Chill completely, then remove the solidified fat from the surface of the broth and reserve. Use a ladle to scoop out the broth (it should be clear) and transfer to a separate container, leaving behind any debris.

To serve, bring the broth to a simmer and add the mirin and sea salt. Taste and adjust seasoning as you like. Grill the chicken thighs, or poach them in the simmering broth until cooked through, about 15 minutes, then leave to cool and slice into chopstick-friendly strips.

Prepare a large saucepan full of boiling water. Melt the fat from the broth in a small saucepan. Cook the noodles in the boiling water according to the package instructions, ensuring that they have a good bite to them. Drain well. Divide the broth evenly among the 4 bowls, then place the noodles in the broth. Top each bowl with a slice of lemon, some sliced chicken thigh, the mizuna, spring onions and a little black pepper. Place the nori squares on the side of each bowl, slightly submerged in the broth.

東
京
モ
ダ
ン

Where to find
Afuri Multiple locations, afuri.com

5F
4F
3F
2F
1F
B1F
B2F

NARISAWA 'BREAD OF THE FOREST' WITH 'MOSS' BUTTER

240

Yoshihiro Narisawa trained in high-end kitchens across central Europe for years before returning to Japan to open his eponymous restaurant in Aoyama in 2003. Ever since, it has consistently been named as not only one of the best restaurants in Tokyo, but one of the best restaurants in the world. It's easy to see why. Narisawa's cooking is an elegant balancing act, between strong and subtle, Japanese and European, classical and modern, but always intensely focused on top-quality produce. While most of Narisawa's dishes are simply presented, he does not shy away from tableside theatre, which he deploys perhaps most strikingly in a course usually presented with no fanfare whatsoever: bread and butter. Narisawa's 'bread of the forest' is first delivered to the table as uncooked dough, which is set in a glass above a small candle. The heat from the candle proves the dough as the menu progresses, until it mushrooms up over the top of the glass, ready for baking. Waiting staff then remove the dough and shape it into small rolls before baking it at the table in a hot stone bowl set between two planks of wood. The bread is infused with yuzu peel and kinome leaves, giving the rolls a fresh, woodsy aroma, and it is served with butter encased in a dehydrated olive paste dusted with chlorophyll, to resemble moss. The whole process is almost like a little play in three acts – proving, baking and eating – and it really is quite a show, transforming the boring bread course into something dramatic and exciting.

MAKES 4 ROLLS WITH 4 PATS OF BUTTER

150 g (5 oz) good-quality black olives, stoned and roughly chopped
80 g (3 oz) good-quality unsalted butter
1 teaspoon caster (superfine) sugar
1 teaspoon dry yeast
120 ml (4 fl oz/½ cup) warm water
120 g (4 oz/1 cup) strong bread flour
80 g (3 oz/⅔ cup) chestnut flour, plus extra for dusting
zest of 1 green yuzu, finely grated
leaves from 2 sprigs of kinome, finely chopped
½ teaspoon salt
about 10 g (½ oz) spinach powder
a few small sprigs flat-leaf parsley

METHOD

Roughly chop the black olives and place on a tray in an oven set to 60°C (140°F) for about 6 hours, until they have a fudgy, dense consistency. Mash the olives into a thick paste using a mortar and pestle or food processor. Shape the butter into 4 small, stone-shaped mounds and place in the fridge until chilled. Spread the olive paste on the surface of the butter to produce little olive butter rocks. Refrigerate until ready to serve.

Stir together the sugar, yeast and warm water until the sugar and yeast dissolve. Combine the flours, yuzu zest, kinome and salt in a bowl or stand mixer. Add the yeast mixture and mix well. Then knead a few times, dusting with a little extra chestnut flour if you're kneading on your countertop (the dough will be very loose and sticky). Place the dough in a glass bowl and leave to prove. The dough is ready to bake when it's doubled in size and very bubbly. Divide the dough into 4 equal-sized rolls.

Heat a stone bowl in a very hot oven for an hour, until the bowl is extremely hot. Remove the bowl and place on a plank of wood. Place the rolls in the bowl and top with another plank of wood. Leave to bake in the hot stone bowl for 12–15 minutes. Or you can just heat your oven to 200°C (400°F/gas 6) and bake the rolls in there on a tray for the same amount of time. Meanwhile, remove the olive butter from the fridge.

Serve the rolls piping hot on a plate with the little olive butter stones on one side. Sprinkle some spinach powder on the olive butter for a 'moss' effect, and place a few leaves of parsley sticking out of the top of each moss-butter mound.

東京モダン

Where to find
Narisawa Aoyama Itchome, 〒107-0062, narisawa-yoshihiro.com

GLOSSARY

If you're cooking these recipes
somewhere outside of Japan, it's
very unlikely you'll have a nearby
depachika to pop into for ingredients.
But that's okay, because Japanese
ingredients are surprisingly easy to
come by these days. The vast majority
of Japanese staples - including soy
sauce, miso, sake, mirin, rice vinegar
and rice - can now be found at most big
supermarkets. For everything else, I'd
recommend shopping online. There's an
enormous wealth of Japanese ingredients
available on the internet, from
well-known super-retailers like Amazon
and eBay or from smaller independent
businesses, and delivery charges
are often less than you might think -
and sometimes free. You can even order
sashimi-grade fish online and have it
delivered in a cool box packed with dry
ice. That's actually amazing! So even if
you're way out of reach of the nearest
Japanese food supplier, Japanese cooking
is still within your grasp.

GOD BLESS THE INTERNET.

aonori
green seaweed flakes

beni shoga
red pickled ginger

bento
lunchbox

conbini
glorious Japanese
convenience stores

daikon
large white radish

dashi
Japanese broth made from
dried kelp and smoked
tuna flakes

depachika
Japanese department store
basement food halls

doubanjiang
Sichuan chilli-bean
paste, a common Chinese
ingredient in Tokyo

Edo
former name of Tokyo

enoki
small, long,
thin mushrooms

eringi
big, meaty king
oyster mushrooms

furikake
Japanese rice seasoning

gochujang
Korean chilli paste

gyoza
Japanese potsticker
dumplings

hijiki
nutty-tasting seaweed,
commonly sold dried

ikura
salt-cured salmon roe

iriko
dried sardines (also
called niboshi)

izakaya
Japanese bars that
serve a range of
drinking snacks

kabocha
very sweet, orange-
fleshed Japanese squash

kabosu
a small, pungent Japanese
lime-like fruit

kaiseki
traditional high-end
Japanese multi-course
meals

kamaboko
fish cakes

katsuobushi
dried smoked
tuna shavings

Kewpie mayo
a particularly
delicious brand of
Japanese mayonnaise

kimchi
spicy fermented
Korean cabbage

kinome
fragrant young leaves of
the Japanese pepper tree

kizami-nori
shredded nori seaweed

koikuchi
rich soy sauce

koji
Japanese mould used to
ferment soy sauce, miso,
sake, etc.

kombu
dried kelp

konnyaku
low-calorie, high-fibre,
rubbery starch jelly

menma
pickled bamboo shoots,
a common ramen topping

mitsuba
mellow Japanese herb

245

mizuna
light leafy greens in
the mustard family

mochi
chewy pounded rice cakes

myoga
fragrant edible flower
in the ginger family

namasu
very lightly
vinegared pickles

naruto
spiral fish cake

natto
sticky fermented soybeans

neta
sushi toppings

niboshi
dried sardines
(also called iriko)

nira
garlic chives

nori
dried seaweed sheets

okonomi sauce
sweet Japanese brown
sauce, typically served
on okonomiyaki

okonomiyaki
Japanese savoury
pancake with a multitude
of fillings

omurice
seasoned rice covered
with an omelette

onigiri
filled Japanese
rice balls

onsen
hot springs

panko
coarse Japanese
breadcrumbs

ponzu
citrus-based seasoning

ramen
alkaline wheat noodles
in meat broth

ramune
Japanese lemonade

sakura-ebi
tiny dried prawns
(shrimp)

sansho
Japanese cultivar of
Sichuan pepper, with
a lemony fragrance

**shichimi/shichimi
togarashi**
a blend of chilli powder
and six other spices

shioyaki
fish semi-cured with
salt, then grilled

shiso
peppery, broad-leafed
Japanese herb

shochu
Japanese distilled spirit

shoyu
soy sauce

soba
buckwheat noodles

somen
very thin wheat noodles

sudachi
a kind of Japanese lime

sukiyaki
beef and vegetable hotpot
with a sweet soy sauce

tamari
very rich soy sauce,
often made with no wheat

tarako
cod's roe

tare
sauce, glaze or other
liquid seasoning

tataki
seared meat or fish,
still raw in the middle

tobiko
flying fish roe

tonkatsu
breaded pork cutlets

tonkatsu sauce
Japanese brown sauce,
typically served
alongside breaded
pork cutlets

tonkotsu
pork broth

tsukune
minced meat patties
or meatballs, typically
chicken

tsuyu
seasoned and concentrated
dashi

udon
thick wheat noodles

umeboshi
very sour, very salty
pickled plums

usukuchi
thin soy sauce

wakame
leafy seaweed,
usually sold dried

washoku
traditional Japanese
cuisine

yoshoku
Western-influenced
Japanese food

yuzu
the one true king
of citrus

yuzu-kosho
paste made from salted
yuzu peel and chillies

INDEX

249

250

251

Acknowledgements

This book is a true collaboration.
It simply would not exist without the
enormous efforts of some seriously
talented people who have been seriously
wonderful to work with: my agent Holly
Arnold, and my publisher Kate Pollard,
who coordinated the entire project with
effortless efficiency; our photographer
Nassima Rothacker, who lugged weighty
equipment through the rain, 32ºC heat
and 90% humidity of Tokyo in September
to capture some truly stunning images
(not to mention the beautiful shots she
took in the studio); our designer Evi O,
who brought order out of the chaos that
is Tokyo in a way that no other designer
could; and the editorial and marketing
teams at Hardie Grant, who have shaped
this project into a gorgeous work of
publishing art. And of course, I must
thank my family for their constant love
and encouragement, especially my wife
Laura, who even let me jet off to Japan
to work on this book while she looked
after our five-month-old baby. Finally,
thank you to my cat, Baloo, for being
an eternally calming presence in a world
filled with uncertainty and stress –
except for that time you got stuck under
the deck.

About the Author

Tim Anderson is executive chef-owner of
the Japanese soul food restaurant Nanban
in Brixton. He is also a MasterChef
champion, a regular contributor to BBC
Radio 4's *The Kitchen Cabinet* and the
author of *JapanEasy* and *Nanban: Japanese
Soul Food*. His affinity for Japanese
food began when he first watched *Iron
Chef* as a teenager; that affinity
developed into a full-on obsession when
at age 18 he moved to Los Angeles to
study Japanese history, and then to
Fukuoka for a two-year working holiday.
He currently resides in Lewisham, south
London, with his wife Laura, daughter
Tig and FIV-positive cat Baloo.

NARA

Published in 2019 by Hardie Grant Books,
an imprint of Hardie Grant Publishing

Hardie Grant Books (London)
5th & 6th Floors
52–54 Southwark Street
London SE1 1UN

Hardie Grant Books (Melbourne)
Building 1, 658 Church Street
Richmond, Victoria 3121

hardiegrantbooks.com

British Library Cataloguing-in-Publication Data. A catalogue record
for this book is available from the British Library.

Tokyo Stories by Tim Anderson
ISBN: 978-1-78488-229-7

Publishing Director: Kate Pollard
Junior Editor: Eila Purvis
Art Direction: Evi O. Studio
Editor: Wendy Hobson
Proofreader: Kay Delves
Photographer: Nassima Rothacker
Food Stylist: Wei Tang
Indexer: Cathy Heath

Colour Reproduction by p2d
Printed and bound in China by Leo Paper Group

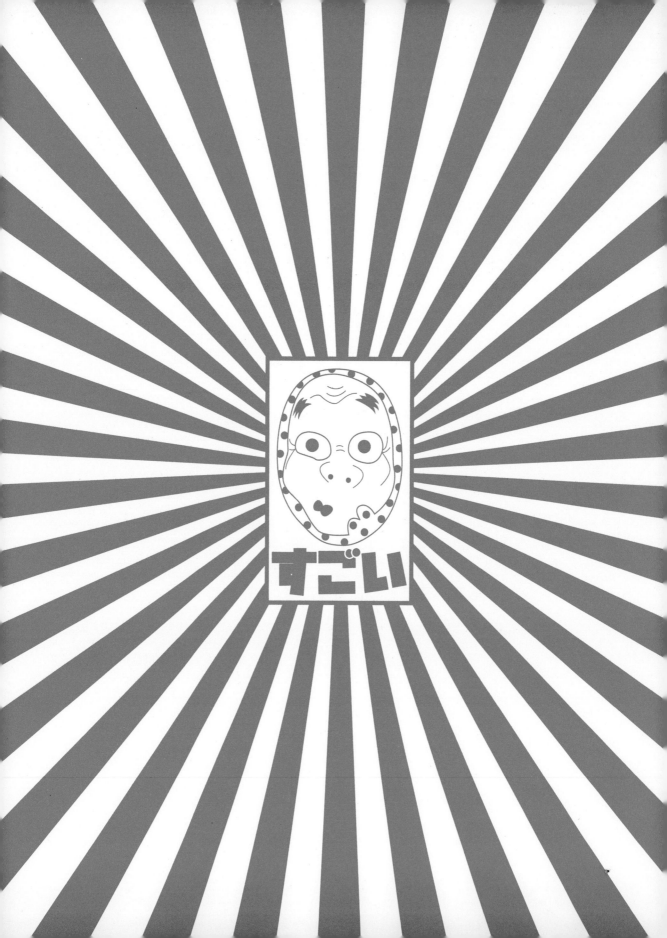